Endorsements

"Like a doctor examining his patient, in *CEO of SELF*, Herman Cain puts life on the examining table. In reading this book, you might conclude that someone else is in charge of you. If so, 'resignations are in order.'"

Cameron M. Alexander, Pastor
Antioch Baptist Church North
Atlanta, Georgia

"Whether on payrolls, self-employed or still in school, many complain about those 'in charge.' But, as Herman Cain points out in his mind-pushing book, they forget— or never realized—who the real bosses are: *themselves.* Read Cain and grow."

Nancy Belck
Chancellor
University of Nebraska at Omaha

"Want to succeed in business and in life? In simple, readable, compelling prose, Herman Cain tells you how. Take his advice to heart—this man has the credentials and experience to give it!"

Steve Forbes
President & CEO
Editor-in-Chief, Forbes
Presidential Candidate (2000)

"Herman Cain applies sound principles of business leadership to inspire personal responsibility for individual success and wellbeing."

Steven F. Goldstone
Former Chairman and Chief Executive
RJR Nabisco

"Herman Cain's book, *CEO of SELF*, is a powerful and inspiring work. It should be required reading for anyone aspiring to be a successful leader."

William H. Gray, III
President and Chief Executive Officer
The College Fund

"Herman Cain gets to the bottom line of having a successful and happy life in *CEO of SELF*. He has translated his success into a commonsense approach for anyone who wants to achieve their dreams."

Richard C. Green, Jr.
Chairman and CEO
UtiliCorp United

"This is not a book about business. It is a book about life. How to balance successfully career, family, and host of other demands and opportunities that we all confront. It is both practical and powerful—because it is a story told by an exceptional, accomplished person."

Irvine O. Hockaday, Jr.
President and Chief Executive Officer
Hallmark Cards

"Many people have figured out how to succeed in business without being able to succeed in life. Herman Cain, a world class entrepreneur, has done both. And, he has the creative gift of being able to share his model of happiness with others in *CEO of SELF: You're in Charge*."

Bob Johnson,
Chairman and Chief Executive Office
BET Holdings

"As Herman Cain says in this inspirational work, 'Life Is About Choices.' I can think of few better choices than this book, with its fresh perspectives and real-life anecdotes, for those hoping to achieve both greater success . . . and greater balance in their busy personal and professional lives."

James M. Kilts
Chairman and CEO
The Gillette Company

"This is a no nonsense guide for getting the most out of one's life. Its pragmatism is embedded in a set of personal and inspirational stories, both instructive and appealing. Herman Cain has done it again."

Walter E. Massey
President
Morehouse College

"This is an inspiring account that traces the ascent of a charismatic corporate CEO. His lessons learned become a guide to success in business but, more importantly, success in life. A call to action and a must read."

Thomas O. Ryder
Chairman and CEO
Reader's Digest

"Wow! I knew Herman Cain was a possibility thinker, but I *now* know he must have been born that way. *CEO of SELF, You're in Charge*, is such a compelling message that it will force you to ask yourself the hard questions about your dreams, your success, and your happiness."

Robert H. Schuller
The Crystal Cathedral
Author of Possibility Thinking

"From his successful personal and professional life, Herman Cain has developed an inspiring, compelling formula for successful leadership and personal fulfillment. It is truly inspiring and shows how to call upon one's inner sources of creativity, strength and courage—characteristics needed by true leaders."

Louis W. Sullivan, M.D.
President, Morehouse School of Medicine
U.S. Secretary of Health and Human
Services, 1989-1993

"'The man's not human,' or so I thought after witnessing first hand the powerful effect he can have on an audience. After coming to know the man and reading *CEO of SELF*, he reveals that he is indeed human and opens wide in this book, the very essence of his humanity."

Timothy P. Taft
President and COO
Whataburger Incorporated

CEO of SELF

CEO *of* SELF

YOU'RE IN CHARGE!

by

Herman Cain

Tapestry Press

Irving, Texas

Tapestry Press
3649 Conflans Road
Suite 103
Irving, TX 75061

Printed in the United States of America

05 04 03 02 01 5 4 3 2 1

Library of Congress Cataloging-in-Publication Data
Cain, Herman.
  CEO of self : you're in charge! / by Herman Cain.
    p. cm.
  1. Cain, Herman. 2. Restaurateurs—United States—Biography. 3.
Happiness. I. Title.
TX910.5.C29 A3 2001
647.95'092—dc21

                              2001005189

Book design and layout by
D. & F. Scott Publishing, Inc.
North Richland Hills, Texas

Cover design by Reneé Rivera, Leopard, Inc.

To my grandmother,
Fannie Lou Davis,
who was CEO of SELF
until the age of 104.

Contents

Contents

Acknowledgments

Many, many thanks to:

Gloria, Melanie and Vincent for giving me three reasons to succeed.

Melanie and Cesare, whose marriage gave us our first granddaughter, Celena Patrice, who added even more joy to this wonderful adventure called life.

Kathleen Sullivan, chief operating officer of T.H.E. Inc., for challenging me to write this book, by suggesting that professional writers have at least three books.

Sibby Wolfson, my executive assistant, for bringing her editorial skills out of the closet to pre-edit the manuscript, and for her valuable critique of content.

Bruce Bortz, my editor, for forcing me to focus and challenging me to dig deep inside of myself to reveal more of my feelings than I thought I could.

Jill Bertolet, my publisher, a valuable member of our team.

The thousands of people who have heard me speak, and have inspired me in return.

Herman Cain

Introduction

Think of yourself as the chief executive officer (CEO) of a company called SELF, Incorporated. As the CEO, you are responsible for SELF's vision (dreams), as well as its operating strategy (how it will achieve its goals and vision).

As SELF's CEO, your job is to also obtain and allocate the resources (money) necessary to operate the company as it grows toward its vision, and to surround yourself with the right people (family and friends) to help you get there. That's what CEOs do.

The other key part of the CEO's job description is to enhance shareholder value. SELF, Inc.'s shareholders are you, your immediate family, your parents and siblings, and your employer.

Your immediate family is a shareholder because of the commitment between husband and wife, and the joint responsibility for the decision to have children, if children are decided on.

Your parents are shareholders because they invested in you to help you get started in life, and they deserve some return on their investment, which may be obtained in various ways.

If you have sisters and brothers, they have a vested interest in you because, with you, they share the later-life responsibility to care for, and provide companionship to, your parents. Love is a bonus, because it keeps you from killing family members when they get on your last nerve.

The company you work for is a shareholder because your employer needs you to help add value to the company, or they would not be paying you to be there. This in turn allows you to earn money to care for your primary shareholders (you and your family).

To succeed, a CEO must be a leader. The only question is whether he or she is a good leader or a great leader. In either case, there are a few critical things you must do to achieve any level of success. The better you do them, the more you will achieve, and the more value you will generate for all of your shareholders—starting with you, because you are the largest shareholder.

It follows, therefore, that in order to provide maximum shareholder value to your family and to other shareholders, the health, happiness, and well-being of the CEO of SELF must be a top priority. This does not suggest excessive selfishness, but it does suggest giving yourself permission to obtain your fair share of value for SELF, Inc. CEOs are usually the best compensated.

Those who are not chief executive officer (CEO) of SELF, Inc. can be called second in command (SIC), which is pronounced "sick." If you are not CEO of SELF, you are SIC of SELF or something less. The lower you are in the chain of command of SELF, Inc., the more you're likely to be abdicating your responsibilities as the CEO. When that happens, you are not maximizing value for all of your stockholders, because your success and happiness, by default, are being determined by a committee. It is perfectly normal for various stockholders to give advice if you ask them to serve on your "board of directors," but the CEO must make the final decisions and provide the leadership in order for SELF, Inc. to be truly successful and happy.

This book is about principles I have used throughout my career and life, long before I was giving keynote speeches or writing books. As I ultimately became CEO of various businesses, and was invited to join the board of directors of some of America's greatest corporations, I discovered that the principles of successful leadership in the business world are the *same* as those that allowed me to succeed as CEO of SELF.

As I began sharing these principles with audiences in keynote speeches on leadership, the feedback was so profound that I felt compelled to write them down. Thousands of people have heard me speak on "Leadership Is Common Sense," which defines CEO of SELF, and hundreds have told me or written me that it changed their life.

As Dr. Robert Schuller says, "If you can dream it, you can go from nowhere to anywhere." You certainly ought to be able to go from where you are today to where you want to be tomorrow as a renewed, reinvigorated, and refocused CEO of SELF.

1

Success Starts Somewhere

The Road Is Not Straight

The road to success and happiness is not straight.
There's a curve called failure,
A loop called confusion,
Speed bumps called friends,
Caution lights called family,
Red lights called enemies, and
Jobs that go flat.
But with a spare called determination,
An engine called perseverance,
Insurance called faith, and
A driver called God,
You will make it to a place called
Success and happiness.

—Unknown

Success Starts Somewhere

A Bumpy Start

I have felt in charge of my life since I was sixteen years old. I did not call myself CEO of SELF then, but that was how I felt, because it was then that I set for myself my first major goal in life—earning $20,000 a year in salary. I did not know how or when I would achieve such a goal, but that became my dream. I had heard or read somewhere that you needed an annual income of ten thousand dollars a year to qualify for an American Express charge card. I did not want to just qualify, I wanted to more than qualify. And I thought $20,000 a year in income would provide a very comfortable lifestyle, one where I would not have to work three jobs like my Dad to live comfortably.

I can still remember driving home from my part-time job working in my father's small neighborhood grocery store when I got what then seemed like this very wild idea of earning $20,000 a year. At the time I formulated this extremely bold dream, I also had no idea what profession I wanted to pursue, because there was not a lot of talk in our house about what we should be when we grew up. We did talk about being able to get a good job to make a lot of money, and $20,000 was a whole lot of money to a sixteen year-old in 1961.

Both Mom and Dad encouraged my brother and me to go to school and to get a good education, because the more education we got, they told us, the better the job. Both Mom and Dad were able to get only a limited amount of formal education when they were growing up. Mom had gotten through the eighth grade before she left her father's small farm in Georgia, and Dad made it through a small town high school in Tennessee.

> **No one in my family had ever gone beyond high school.**

Our high school teachers stressed getting a good education if we wanted to be successful, and they also encouraged us to pursue college and a professional career. At the time, the whole idea of going to college and becoming a professional "anything" seemed so un-achievable, since no one in my family had ever gone beyond high school, and since segregation and discrim-ination "red lights," as in the chapter opening poem, were still legal. How could I believe I could become an engineer or corporate vice president with a vivid daily reminder printed in large black letters across the front of the public transportation buses: "White seat from front, colored seat from rear"?

When I was thirteen, my friends and I were riding home from school one day aboard a bus that was far from full. As soon as a few white passengers boarded, the bus driver asked us to move to the back of the bus. Though we knew this was "the way it was," it was still an insult to our dignity each and every time it happened. We also knew that things were heating up in the South, with sit-ins and bus boycotts and some police officers just looking for a reason to shoot a black person who "got out of line," so we chose to move to the back of the bus, rather than get into trouble.

Charles S. Johnson was my home-room teacher and mathematics teacher for all five years of high school. He encouraged me to go to college and to major in mathematics, and he told me that I could decide later what profession I might pursue. Mr. Johnson also told me that I could be whatever I wanted to be, but that I might have to *work a little harder, and work a little longer*, to get there. My high school band teacher, Mr. Lloyd Terry, also constantly encouraged me—as well as the others in the band—to be the best because we had the ability to be the best. He wasn't just referring to our instrument playing, but to all of our aspirations.

Mr. Johnson, Mr. Terry, and my Dad also suggested that college would help me make a lot of money, so college was definitely part of my game plan, and Dad and Mr. Johnson and Mr. Terry were definitely influential members of my board of SELF, Inc.

I applied to, and was accepted by, several historically black colleges, and was even offered scholarships to most of them, because of my rank as salutatorian of my graduating class (second highest grades). I certainly was not offered the scholarships based on my standardized test scores, because they were consistently mediocre, as were the scores of most of my classmates.

In my case, I believe this was mostly due to poor reading habits while growing up. My parents never read to us as children, and they never insisted that we read books outside of schoolwork, so my reading skills at the time always lagged behind where they should have been ("speed bump"). Fortunately, when I entered Morehouse College, I was required to take a semester-long reading course to get my reading skills closer to where a college freshman's should be. Fifty percent of the entering freshmen had to take this course, which definitely helped. Yet, I believe I didn't really catch up to my reading level even then, which is why I struggled in all my college courses except for math and science.

I had decided to attend Morehouse College because it was affordable. Because of its Atlanta location, I could commute by bus from home. Morehouse also awarded me a first-year tuition scholarship, which could be renewed if I maintained a B average or better in my classes. The scholarship was not renewed at the end of my freshman year, which was another little "speed bump" I had to deal with. Although I was disappointed, I never felt defeated because I knew I had worked as hard as I could. But to help pay the tuition from then on, I worked various part-time jobs, during school and during summers, and Mom and Dad helped with the rest.

At the time I began college, I was not familiar with Morehouse's reputation as a great institution of higher learning, nor had I ever heard of Dr. Benjamin E. Mays, its president. For every young man who attended Morehouse, he was a demanding educator, an inspiring leader, and an even more inspiring member of their personal boards of directors. Consider his charge to us: "There is an air of expectancy at Morehouse College. It is expected that the student who enters here will do well. It is also expected that once a man bears the insignia of a Morehouse graduate, he will do exceptionally well. We expect nothing less."

My high school teacher, Mr. Johnson, was a Morehouse graduate, as was Willie Harding, a friend at church. Both of them had encouraged me to go to "The House," as it was affectionately called by people who knew of its reputation.

> **It's not a calamity to die with dreams unfulfilled, but it is a calamity to have no dreams.**

My decision to attend Morehouse was one of the best decisions I ever made, not just because of the great education I received there, but also because of the great inspiration it provided me from three different sources: the fact that it was all male and all black, the fact that so many of its graduates had done so many great things following graduation, and the fact that its president was Dr. Mays. He not only had high expectations of his graduates, but he instilled in me and many others one of the larger truths I've followed throughout my life: *"It's not a calamity to die with dreams unfulfilled, but it is a calamity to have no dreams."*

Later in my life, I would learn that this is, and should be, the mantra for the true CEO of SELF.

Before deciding to attend Morehouse, I had also applied to the University of Georgia (UGA) and Georgia Institute of Technology (Georgia Tech), both of which denied me admission. In 1963, when I graduated from high school and started college, these two state-funded institutions had been desegregated for only two years. The number of black students they admitted was still being kept to a minimum. Although I am not sure if I would have attended either school had I been admitted, I would have liked having that choice.

A generation later, our daughter Melanie did have that choice, and to this day I do not know for certain why she was so determined to attend the University of Georgia, because we were living in Nebraska at the time. I suspect her decision to attend UGA, from which she graduated in 1994, had something to do with an option I didn't have, and that makes us proud of her in more ways than one.

> **I clearly am a benefi-
> ciary of the civil rights
> movement of the 50s
> and 60s.**

When I graduated from Morehouse in 1967, I was fairly typical of a graduate from a historically black college. The Civil Rights Act of 1964 had opened a lot of doors in corporate America and in government, which gave us opportunities our parents could only have dreamed about. I clearly am a beneficiary of the civil rights movement of the 50s and 60s.

In 1967, I received twenty-five formal job offers from some of America's most successful and respected corporations, and I was only a C+ student overall, with just a B average in my major, which was mathematics. I started my career with the Department of the Navy making $7,729 per year, but I knew that with hard work and long hours, I was on my way to earning $20,000 per year . . . and achieving my dream!

I have realized for a long time how fortunate I was to have had Mom and Dad, Dr. Mays, Mr. Johnson, and

Mr. Terry, in my life. Collectively, they gave me my real start in life. They taught me to believe in God, to believe in myself, and to believe that I could accomplish anything my heart desired.

Poor reading skills, an inability to keep my scholarship in college, and the disadvantages of discrimination created a bumpy start for this future CEO, but they were not enough to defeat my determination and perseverance. I could have chosen to drop out of college when I lost my scholarship, and I could have chosen to use discrimination as an excuse to settle for the first job that came my way.

As CEO of SELF, I chose to graduate from Morehouse College, which gave me the opportunity to choose from twenty-five great job offers. I chose to stay focused on my dream.

Unmarked Curves

Whenever my Dad and Mom took my brother and me to Arlington, Tennessee, to visit the small dirt farm where Dad grew up, Dad would always drive. As we got closer to that little farmhouse near Memphis, Dad would have to leave the main paved highway, and take some narrow unpaved roads. Off the regular highway, the road curves were not well marked, and Dad would have to be extra careful, because he never knew when another car or truck might be coming at us from the opposite direction.

Segregation and discrimination were "well- marked" when I graduated from college and I knew exactly what to expect. But when I moved to Dahlgren, Virginia to work for the Department of the Navy as a GS-7 mathematician, and began my climb from $7,729 a year to $20,000 a year, I nonetheless encountered some unmarked and unexpected curves. The first was trying to get a haircut, and the second was unequal pay for the same performance.

I have often told the story of how, in 1967, I wanted to get a haircut and had to drive to the nearby town of Fredericksburg, Virginia, because I did not know of any barbershops in the small town of Dahlgren. When I got to Fredericksburg, I drove around town until I finally saw a barbershop with some black barbers. I parked my car and went in, sat down, and waited for one of the barbers to let me know when I was next. This was the custom while growing up in Atlanta, and I knew it well—my Dad had also been a barber at one time.

> **I sat there for about thirty minutes while everybody was told "next" except for me. I then noticed that I was the only black patron in the shop.**

I sat there for about thirty minutes while everybody was told "next" except for me. I then noticed that I was the only black patron in the shop. I finally asked one of the barbers why they had not called me, and that's when he told me that they were not allowed to cut black people's hair in that shop. I felt like a truck had hit me. The indignities of segregation, I thought, were over, and had mostly been experienced in the South. This was seventy miles south of Washington, D.C. I later wondered why they allowed me to sit there for thirty minutes without telling me what was going on. In fact, if I had not asked, I might still be sitting there . . . waiting to be "next."

Another story I have related previously is that my white, Navy co-worker was always getting promoted one month earlier than I was, even though we were both consistently receiving outstanding ratings on our performance reviews. One day, I *asked* my boss why, and he said it was because I did not have a master's degree, and my co-worker did. Again, I would not have known the real story unless I had asked.

> **As CEO of SELF, you always have choices to make. In both of these situations, I chose to *remove the barriers* rather than allow the barriers to remove me.**

As CEO of SELF, you always have choices to make. In both of these situations and others during my climb up the corporate ladder, I chose to *remove the barriers* rather than allow the barriers to remove me. I left the barbershop that day and bought a set of hair clippers to cut my own hair. I have been cutting it ever since. This was not just an act of defiance and necessity, but it also turned out to be tremendously convenient. My grandmother referred to this as "making lemonade when life deals you a lemon."

The barrier called "lack of a master's degree" took a lot longer to remove. I had worked at the Dahlgren facility for three years before I was able to go back to graduate school. I attended Purdue and earned a master's degree in computer science. Shortly after my return to work in my fifth year of employment, a GS-13 supervisory position became available and I was offered the position. The salary was $20,001 per year!

Success is a journey with many unmarked curves. As the CEO of SELF, I had to ask the right questions, and then make a choice between removing the barrier, going around the barrier, or allowing the barrier to remain between me and my dream.

2

The Chauffeur's Son

Still I Rise

You may write me down in history
With your bitter twisted lies,
You may trod me in the very dirt
But still, like dust, I'll rise.
Just like moons and like suns,
With the certainty of tides,
Just like hopes springing high,
Still I'll rise.
You may shoot me with your words,
You may cut me with your eyes,
You may kill me with your hatefulness,
But still, like air, I'll rise.

—Maya Angelou

(Excerpts from her poem "Still I Rise"
The Complete Collected Poems of Maya Angelou
Random House Publishers)

The Chauffeur's Son

After achieving my first big dream of making $20,000 a year, I realized that I needed a new dream. The initial one had become simply a destination point that I had reached (indeed, with my promotion, I had surpassed it by one dollar). Although I enjoyed my new position as GS-13 supervisory mathematician, I gradually became bored. The adventure had been the challenge of getting there. Once I got there, I did not feel much like a CEO of SELF. I felt more like I was "treading water."

> **My father was the chauffeur and personal assistant to the chairman and CEO of The Coca-Cola Company.**

My father had worked most of his career at The Coca-Cola Company in Atlanta. When he was not chauffeuring around a company executive, he assisted in the executive dining room at the company's headquarters and saw the life of corporate executives up-close and personal. As Dad moved up in the chauffeur's ranks at the company, he was eventually asked to be the full-time chauffeur and personal assistant to the chairman and CEO of the company, R. W. Woodruff. This was a coveted position among Dad's fellow workers, even though it was a "24/7" job most of the time.

When Mr. Woodruff went out of town, Dad did not have to go with him, so he would have that time off from work. Dad used to share a lot with my brother and me about what he observed being around high-level executives so much, and even though Dad never told us anything "out of school" or confidential, he saw and heard a lot.

> **One day, I said out loud. "I want to be vice president of something for somebody, somewhere, someday."**

My image of a corporate executive came mostly from my Dad's experiences, from magazines, and from TV. I did not personally know anyone who was CEO, president, or vice president of *anything*, though I imagined that such CEOs made a lot of money and enjoyed both social prestige and a nice lifestyle. One day, this image became my dream and I said it out loud. "I want to be vice president of something for somebody, somewhere, someday." This meant that I had to leave my job with the government, because vice president of the United States was not what I had in mind.

I put together my résumé and, as a courtesy to my Dad, was given an interview with The Coca-Cola Company. Bob Copper, who headed a corporate analysis group in Atlanta, conducted the interview, but informed me right from the start that no jobs were available. I thanked him for his honesty, and we had a great talk anyway.

About two weeks later, Bob called me and asked if I would return for a visit with his boss and a couple of other people. When I asked why, he said I had exceeded his expectations during our meeting, and he was trying to convince his boss to create a position for me. He succeeded, and I came aboard.

Climbing the Corporate Ladder

The position at Coca-Cola challenged my analytical and communication skills, and even though the company salary was basically the same as what I had been earning with the federal government, this lateral move gave me an opportunity to work in a corporation and to get some exposure to business. Although I had the title of manager of management science, I was actually a project manager, like other members of the group Bob headed up. For four years, I worked on some very interesting projects, and learned the basic concepts and language of business. The Coca-Cola position proved to be a great starting point in what for me was the still somewhat unknown world of corporate America.

> For four years, I worked on some very interesting projects, and learned the basic concepts and language of business.

Bob Copper was a great boss He had a knack for making his group a fun group to work in, while still accomplishing great results. Bob was also a great CEO of SELF. Although he, too, had had a "bumpy start" in life, he was determined to achieve his dreams. One was to become a corporate vice president someday.

> *I have always been more motivated by the possibility of success than the fear of failure.*

The Pillsbury Company in Minneapolis hired Bob about three years after I started at Coca-Cola, and not long after that he invited me to join his group at Pillsbury. While at Coca-Cola, Bob had assembled a very competent group of guys, many of whom had worked for him a lot longer than I had, so I wanted to know why he'd offered *me* the Pillsbury job. He told me it was because I was more of a risk taker than the others, and there was some risk in what he was trying to accomplish at Pillsbury. After he told me what he was supposed to accomplish, I asked what would happen if "we" did not succeed. He said "we" would then be looking for new jobs. The comment did not scare me off. *I have always been more motivated by the possibility of success than the fear of failure.*

I accepted the Pillsbury offer with Bob, but this time it came with a sizeable increase in compensation. I even received some stock options, which I had never heard of before. I started as manager of business analysis, and this time I had some people to manage.

Bob and I were both very successful at Pillsbury, and, as a result, were assigned more and more responsibility. In a few short years, I moved from manager to director, from director to group director, and from group director to senior director of Management Information Systems for the Consumer Products Division. Until he became vice president of strategic planning for Pillsbury, I reported to Bob, and then I reported to Dr. John Haaland, who was the corporate vice president of systems for Pillsbury. John was also a great guy to work for because he did not try to over-manage, and we had a great working relationship.

When John (another true CEO of SELF) decided to leave Pillsbury to pursue an entrepreneurial adventure, he called me—I was attending an out of town conference at the time—to let me know that I had been selected to replace him as vice president of corporate systems. I said, "Did you say vice president?" John said, "Yes."

> **Why not dream even higher—of being *p-p-p-president* of something, somewhere, for somebody, someday?**

While serving several years as vice president of corporate systems and services, I successfully completed some major initiatives for the company, and things were running smoothly. I once again felt I needed more challenge, and now that I was an accomplished vice president, why not dream even higher—of being *p-p-p-president* of something, somewhere, for somebody, someday? So I did.

Achieving this dream, however, required a major career change, because even though I was running a very important staff function for Pillsbury, I did not have profit and loss (P & L) responsibility for a business unit.

On the advice of Win Wallin, the president of Pillsbury and my boss, I explored the possibility of going to work for Burger King, Inc., a Pillsbury subsidiary at the time. Win's premise was that if I wanted someday to become president of a business unit, one of Pillsbury's restaurant companies was the most likely candidate since they were all growing so rapidly.

After meeting with the president of Burger King and some of its executives, I was offered an opportunity to enter their "fast track" program, since I had no operations experience. If I completed the eighteen-month program successfully, I could be made vice president and regional general manager. It was a highly coveted position in Burger King, because even though you reported to an executive vice president at BK headquarters in Miami, it came with full P & L responsibility for a region of the country, and in your region you were "the man."

> **I entered BK's fast track program, knowing the move to Burger King required a cut in pay, loss of stock options, working irregular hours (including weekends), and learning a new business.**

I entered BK's fast track program, knowing the move to Burger King required a cut in pay, loss of stock options, working irregular hours (including weekends), learning a new business, and learning the operation from A to Z. These were not problems, because I knew about them up front. The real challenge came later, overcoming what I didn't anticipate: resentment, sabotage, and a conspiracy to get me fired!

In retrospect, not anticipating these obstacles may have been a blessing in disguise, because had I expected them up front, I might have lost sight of my dream. Instead, I focused on the problems as they came to light. *That's what CEOs do all the time—solve problems so they can move on and stay focused.*

> **That's what CEOs do all the time—solve problems so they can move on and stay focused.**

The resentment came from the fact that, as a former vice president with the parent company, Pillsbury, I was going to deny a Burger King veteran one of the coveted regional positions. Never mind the fact that Burger King's top management wanted to broaden the experience base of its regional VPs, or that tenure alone was no guarantee for success.

The sabotage happened when I became a restaurant manager for the first time. One of the duties of a closing manager is to tie out the register receipts with the actual cash on hand. You'd then balance out these amounts, take your deposit to the bank, keeping enough to start business the next day. I'd been at this particular restaurant about a month or two when one night, one of the assistant managers purposely removed fifty dollars from the store's cash receipts to cause the daily settlement report to be short. It was short by exactly fifty dollars.

I stayed there all night trying to figure out what was wrong, counting and re-counting and re-counting, asking myself if I'd done something wrong or if the record tapes were incorrect. It drove me nuts! I didn't leave until the opening manager for the next day arrived. I finally gave up and reported the shortage on my daily report. I closed the following night and guess what happened? Now, the cash was fifty dollars *over*, which I also indicated on my report. It was a setup designed to shake me up and to see if I would go strictly according to procedure. I was made aware of the resentment and the intentional shell game with the fifty dollars during my last week as restaurant manager.

> **The assistant manager who removed and then replaced the fifty dollars confessed and apologized to me for what he had done. He felt bad about it because he had come to respect me for what I had done to help the restaurant succeed, and for my sincerity when dealing with people.**

The assistant manager who removed and then replaced the fifty dollars confessed and apologized to me for what he had done. He felt bad about it because he had come to respect me for what I had done to help the restaurant succeed, and for my sincerity when dealing with people. I accepted his apology, and then went on to talk about what he wanted to do with his life as CEO of SELF, *and* we remained friends. He also explained that it was common knowledge throughout the Minneapolis region that the vice president of the region wanted me to fail. This was confirmed independently, in an unsolicited way, by several other people working in the region.

Three months after I became manager of that first restaurant, its sales increased by 20 percent. After only nine months in the fast track program, instead of the original eighteen months, I was pulled out and appointed region vice president (RVP) of the Philadelphia Region.

> **Three months after I became manager of that first restaurant, its sales increased by 20 percent.**

A new conspiracy to get me fired played out during my tenure as VP of the Philadelphia Region. It involved my Pillsbury background, a direct report, a franchisee, and a higher-level officer of Burger King who felt threatened by my performance. Following a reassignment of region reporting relationships, my new boss, Bill DeLeat, then an executive vice president of BKC Corporate, came to visit my region to determine first-hand how things were going. The financials were all exceeding our annual targets, but as Bill put it, "There are a lot of people in Miami (corporate headquarters) who do not like you and want you fired."

I felt crushed, since after only a year and a half as RVP, my region was exceeding its performance goals. After spending about three intensive days in my region,

Bill also told me that it was unquestionably one of the best regions, if not *the* best region, in the company.

Bill started a campaign in Corporate to correct the unfair and inaccurate perception of my performance. He could have chosen not to do anything about it, but he was a CEO of SELF, and he had great integrity. Bill DeLeat was one of those angels for whom you can only be thankful, especially when things are so unfair. Since the corporate attitudes toward me were personal, and not performance based, they did not change much, but Bill provided strong support and "watched my back" while I just kept doing my job. If handled differently, the entire episode could have ended my corporate career. Period.

> **After three years of running the Philadelphia Region, the president of Burger King called me about taking over as president of Godfather's Pizza, Inc.**

After three years of running the Philadelphia Region, I received a phone call from Jeff Campbell while attending an RVP meeting in San Francisco, California. Jeff had been president of Burger King before being promoted to an executive position at Pillsbury, where he was in charge of all the restaurant companies. Jeff was my boss's boss's boss, and although I knew him and had a good relationship with him, he didn't have time to be calling me out of a meeting just to say hello. I returned Jeff's call and after the usual small talk, he said he wanted me to meet him in Miami to talk about taking over as president of Godfather's Pizza, Inc., another newly acquired restaurant company. I said, "Did you say president?"

When working at the Department of the Navy, I had had to overcome a lack of advanced educational credentials, so I set a goal of getting a master's degree, and achieved it.

When I moved to The Coca-Cola Company, I had to overcome low expectations (I was, after all, the chauffeur's son), so I was determined to distinguish my performance no matter how hard I had to work.

When I accepted a new job at Pillsbury, I had to overcome the increased risk of failure and the skepticism of those who thought I was a "young whipper-snapper," so I simply never considered failure as an option.

And, when I made a major career change to join Burger King, I had to overcome resentment, sabotage, and a conspiracy.

Other than all that, it was a relatively easy climb up the corporate ladder!

> **When I became president of Godfather's in 1986, I had achieved my wildest dream.**

I'm a CEO

When I became president of Godfather's in 1986, I had achieved my wildest dream. By early 1988, even though Godfather's had regained profitability against the odds, Pillsbury decided to sell Godfather's. I had not yet even conceived another big dream for myself when Ron Gartlan (executive vice president) and I

were presented the opportunity to own the company—
and an opportunity where I would go up one more corporate rung: to CEO.

I had never been fired before in my life, but when I sat
in Jerry Levin's office that day and heard him tell me that
Pillsbury had decided to sell Godfather's, I felt like I had
been fired. All we had done was turn Godfather's from a
losing business to a profitable business in less than eighteen months, and proved all the skeptics wrong. Jerry, who
was Pillsbury's executive vice president of acquisitions
and divestitures, told me that Pillsbury simply did not see
Godfather's as a long-term strategic fit. The pizza segment
of the quick service restaurant industry was growing faster
than the burger segment, but Burger King was "a good strategic fit" and Godfather's wasn't? Go figure.

> **My next dream became
> ownership of a $250
> million business, which
> I did not even fully
> absorb at first because I
> had never before said
> "ownership" out loud.**

Putting together the purchase of Godfather's challenged all of the knowledge and experience that Ron
and I could muster, and even though we had never nav-
igated our way through a buyout before, we felt that
together we could get this one done. Thus, my next
dream became ownership of a $250 million business,
which I did not even fully absorb at first because I had
never before said "ownership" out loud.

The process began in January 1988 and was the most stressful experience of my life. We made presentations of our business plan to eighteen lending institutions, and we had to approach each one with as much enthusiasm as we could generate. Over and over we presented our case, only to receive a polite "No, thank you" a few days later.

But we persevered. As CEO of SELF, I had learned from my parents and grandparents that if one door closes, another door opens, so the best course is to believe in yourself and to look for the next open door instead of focusing on the one just closed. For me, during this agonizing process, the next open door was the next presentation to the next bank. Finally, after our nineteenth presentation, we got a "Yes"! And, as it happened, we were able to close the transaction on September 21, 1988—the very day I became a corporate CEO for the first time.

> As CEO of SELF, I had learned from my parents and grand-parents that if one door closes, another door opens, so the best course is to believe in yourself and to look for the next open door.

When Ron Gartlan, Gary Batenhorst (our general counsel), and I finished signing a ton of documents with Citicorp in New York, we rushed to catch a plane to Tampa, Florida, where months earlier we had scheduled an all-company meeting to present a business update, and, we had hoped, celebrate the change of ownership. We managed that with just a few hours to spare!

When the party ended and I got back to Omaha, Nebraska, Godfather's corporate headquarters, I started to realize the full impact of being CEO of the company. Every decision I made now would not only affect the stockholders of SELF, Inc. and me, but they would also affect all of the Godfather's employees and their families, and all of the franchisees and their employees and families.

I now realized more than ever before the meaning of the expression, "The buck stops here."

When I had been *just* president of Godfather's, and reporting to Pillsbury, Jeff Campbell had served as the CEO. Even though I had a lot of freedom to run the business as I deemed appropriate, Jeff had the final word. I now realized more than ever before the meaning of the expression, "The buck stops here." A friend and former colleague called to congratulate me on the purchase of the company, and asked rhetorically, "So who do you report to now?" Every CEO of SELF must answer that question the same way—"Myself!"—if they expect to achieve success and happiness.

The decision to buy Godfather's was the biggest business decision of my life. I was then forty-two. Despite my bumpy start, I had established a comfortable lifestyle during my climb up the corporate ladder, but I had not accumulated a big savings account. Neither Ron nor I had a rich uncle to back us or to fall back on, so failure was simply not an option. While the banker explained to us the reasons we had to sign a "ton" of documents, he also explained to us his philosophy as a banker, that *before the bank loses a dime, we would lose everything.* Fifteen years later, we still own the company.

I remained as Godfather's CEO until 1996, at which time I became CEO of the National Restaurant Association (NRA). I had been a member of the NRA Board since 1988, and had served as its elected volunteer chairman in 1994/1995. I thus became the only volunteer chairman to become the full-time *paid* CEO of the Association while still a member of the board.

> **I remained as Godfather's CEO until 1996, at which time I became CEO of the National Restaurant Association (NRA).**

This did not come about because I sought the position. It happened because fellow board members asked me to fill the position when it became vacant, because of our accomplishments during my one-year term as volunteer chairman. At first, I declined. If I was going to be CEO, I needed to be in charge. But I later changed my mind when they agreed to make some structural changes that would allow me, despite the association's diverse constituency, to get some important things accomplished. They also agreed that I would remain in the job for only two to three years.

When I was CEO of Godfather's, the board consisted of the two principal owners, Ron and me. When I was CEO of the NRA, the board consisted of seventy-five restaurateurs, all elected by the general membership of the Association from around the country. The board members represented the full range of restaurant categories, such as independent operators, chain operators, operators of full service restaurants, quick service restaurants, and casual dining establishments. They often have different priorities on issues.

For instance, full service operators would want more NRA resources spent on IRS requirements that employers track employee tips, whereas quick service chains would be more concerned about minimum wage legislation because of the industry's large number of entry level workers and the high turnover rate. Additionally, even though each of the fifty State Restaurant Associations were independent organizations, maintaining a great working relationship with each of them was critical to the success of the NRA. Issues negatively affecting the industry could sometimes start out at the state level and then later appear at the federal level, and vice versa.

> **The challenges of working with a very large board and fifty state associations made communications and consensus building extremely demanding.**

At the NRA, the CEO's responsibilities of providing leadership for vision, strategy, resources, and execution were the same as I had as CEO of Godfather's, or at any other organization. But the challenges of working with a

very large board and fifty state associations made communications and consensus building extremely demanding.

I stayed for two and a half years, during which time
we substantially strengthened the Association. We launch-
ed a three-year technology initiative to update the association's systems infrastructure, and established a financial
"war chest" (called SAFE—Save American Free Enter-
prise) that enabled us to respond quickly to major legisla-
tive and regulatory threats to the restaurant industry. And
we were identified by *Fortune* magazine as the fifteenth
most influential association in Washington, D.C. The NRA
had never before even cracked the top 100.

> **In 1998, I was recruited
> to become CEO of
> RetailDNA, a start-up
> technology company.**

In 1998, I was recruited to become CEO of RetailDNA,
a start-up technology company focusing on smart marketing applications for retail businesses. The first target
market for these applications was the restaurant industry, and my mission was to lead the development of the
vision, business strategy, organization, and initial top-
level marketing. I completed my mission in June of 2000,
when I began focusing full-time on T.H.E. Inc., my keynote speaking and leadership consulting company.

As CEO, founder, speaker, writer, and CRG (chief
revenue generator) for T.H.E. Inc., the buck really stops
with me, and fast! But after thirty-five years of climbing
the corporate ladder, serving as CEO of several businesses, and serving on the boards of several Fortune
500 companies, I have discovered one of the greatest

freedoms a person can hope for in his career and life. That freedom is being able to do what you really love doing, while still pursuing your *next* dream—continued success and happiness.

> **One of the greatest freedoms a person can hope for is being able to do what you really love doing.**

As CEO of SELF, the buck stops with you for your success and happiness, no matter how much you delegate that responsibility to others, or simply deny that anyone has that responsibility. You may have some very influential people on the Board of Directors of SELF, such as your spouse or parents, but you have to make the big decisions in your life. Whether it is a big career decision, business decision, or personal decision, it's your call, because *you're in charge.*

The biggest personal decision of my life was when I asked Gloria to marry me, and the biggest personal decision of her life was when she said "yes." Make no mistake about it, we are both CEOs of our respective selves, but we are also vice chairman and vice chairwoman, respectively, of each other's Board of Directors. Mutual advice and support on key decisions and destination points are invaluable. The love we share is priceless.

A Tribute to Thurman

My only brother Thurman was the chauffeur's other son. He made some choices as CEO of SELF that ruined his health and shortened his life.

When growing up, it was just the two of us. Thurman was a year and a half younger than I, and even though we had our fair share of the normal sibling squabbles, we actually enjoyed being with each other and doing things together. We even had a lot of the same friends until he decided to attend the new high school that opened closer to our home. I had already put in three years at S. H. Archer High School, and wanted to finish my last two years there.

> **My only brother Thurman was the chauffeur's other son. He made some choices as CEO of SELF that ruined his health and shortened his life.**

We both had outgoing personalities, and we both enjoyed being around people. I was no wallflower, but Thurman was more of the life of the party. He loved to laugh, and he loved to make others laugh.

But, sometimes his idea of a good laugh got both of us in trouble. One Christmas, when we were about nine and ten, our parents bought us BB guns as presents. We were visiting an aunt, and playing outside her home, when Thurman told an older cousin, Elizabeth, not to move as he pointed his BB gun toward her. She moved and dared him to shoot her, so he shot her right in the butt. She was not badly hurt, but the BB did sting.

Thanks to Thurman, we never saw those BB guns again. Mom took them from both of us forever.

Both of us were also musically inclined. I began learning to play the trombone when I entered the eighth grade, and to my surprise, Thurman also chose the trombone when he entered the eighth grade. I thought he would have selected a different instrument just to be different from me, but in some ways he wanted to be just like his older brother. We both became lead players (first chair) in our respective high school and college bands, as well as senior leaders in our bands.

In addition, we both sang in our church youth choir. I inherited more of my Dad's singing ability and would often be asked to sing solo parts like my Dad, but Thurman—well, let's just say he inherited his singing ability from Mom. We won't go there.

I was more consistent in high school about making the academic honor roll. Thurman would make the honor roll occasionally, but he would never do really poorly in his classes. There was no doubt that he had the ability to consistently make the honor roll. He just chose not to make it a priority.

Thurman graduated from Morris Brown College, which was also located in Atlanta, and started his career after graduation as a computer programmer with the Shell Oil Company in Houston, Texas. A few years later, he moved back to Atlanta as a programmer with The Coca-Cola Company, and did well for a while until he became more and more attracted to the Atlanta nightlife than to his job or his immediate family. When his career started to hit some detours and potholes, he left Coca-Cola and tried several entrepreneurial ventures, none of which resulted in a dependable livelihood.

Looking back, those experiences may have contributed to his choice of alcohol and eventually drug abuse. But despite many self-inflicted problems and disappointments, he never let his situation extinguish his love of living or his joy of people.

> **Thurman did well for a while until he became more and more attracted to the Atlanta nightlife than to his job or his immediate family.**

We both had the same start in life, similar personalities, and many of the same opportunities, because Mom and Dad made every effort to treat us equally. I also believe we had the same perception of success when we were growing up, which was to make a lot of money. As we got older, I accepted the fact that success of any kind requires perseverance and patience (probably in that order), as well as the ability to focus. Thurman was less accepting of this fact. As a result, he made some very different choices as CEO of SELF. An erratic career, two marriages, and two divorces later, Thurman died in 1999 at the age of fifty-two.

I will remember him most for the pride he had for his three daughters, and some of the better choices he made during his all-too-short life. Thurman chose to remain in Atlanta, where he was able to help Dad when his health started to decline because of complications from diabetes. He chose to be the one to take Dad to the hospital for his frequent kidney dialysis treatments, and he chose to be there to assist Mom when she began to experience the limiting effects of multiple sclerosis.

Thurman chose to be a son when Mom and Dad needed him the most, and a brother for whom I will be forever thankful.

The Rearview Mirror

My father was the first great CEO of SELF I ever knew. Even before I knew what leadership was, I saw in my father the self-motivation to work three jobs simultaneously. I saw his risk taking when he bought and then ran a small neighborhood grocery store. And I saw his formidable focus on achieving his dream of a better life. Here was a man who, at age eighteen, had walked off his father's very small dirt farm not knowing where he would end up. He didn't have a job or a car, and he had hardly any money at all. But he had his dreams.

> **My father was the first great CEO of SELF I ever knew.**

Dad knew he couldn't expect success if he stayed on his father's farm, and he believed that there was a job out there somewhere that would give him a start. In Ohio, where he lived only briefly, he met and married my mother. They spent a brief time together in Tennessee, where I was born. Eventually, they settled in Atlanta, Georgia, where I grew up.

Mom's story was a bit like Dad's. She left behind her father's farm in Georgia, and ran away to Ohio, because she knew her dad would not give her—a mere seventeen-year-old—permission to leave, and she was tired of working on the farm.

I was little more than a year old when Mom and Dad moved to Atlanta, where shortly thereafter my brother, Thurman, was born. Mom thought the names "Herman and Thurman" were cute, and those were the ones she and Dad pinned on us. While growing up, we did not think the names were so cute, since we were not twins. But, we would learn as adults that the person makes the name. The name does not make the person.

> **Raising a family in Atlanta in the 1950s and 1960s was not easy, especially given the social and economic challenges of segregation.**

Raising a family in Atlanta in the 1950s and 1960s was not easy, especially given the social and economic challenges of segregation. When Dad walked off his father's farm in 1943, there was no Civil Rights Act, but that did not stop him from declaring his dreams. He wanted a nice home and a good car. He wanted to put his two sons through college. And, if he died before she did, he wanted to leave enough savings to take care of Mom. In fact, he died in 1982 at the age of fifty-six years.

During his life's journey, Dad never spent a lot of time looking in the rearview mirror or wishing he had done a lot of things differently. He just kept moving ahead despite the "speed bumps, red lights, and detours" he encountered—and there were plenty of them.

This was another valuable CEO of SELF lesson I learned from Dad.

As I travel my life's journey, some things grow dimmer and dimmer in my rearview mirror, but Dad's inspiration becomes brighter and brighter.

The chauffeur's son is as proud of the chauffeur as the chauffeur was proud of his son.

3

Impossible Dreams Achieved

We Are Troubled on Every Side

*We are troubled on every side, yet not distressed;
we are perplexed, but not in despair;
persecuted, but not forsaken;
cast down, but not destroyed . . .*
2 Corinthians Chapter 4

Impossible Dreams
Achieved

In football, it's called a touchdown.
In baseball, it's called a run.
In basketball, it's called a basket.
And in both soccer and ice hockey, it's called a goal.

In each game, the objective is the same—before time runs out, score more touchdowns, runs, baskets, or goals than your opponent. If you do, you win. The dream is to win.

Dreams in life may seem impossible. They are not. Impossible dreams are achieved one goal at a time.

Goals are destination points to reach your dreams, when you put yourself in the *right* position to succeed. No one knows how much time we will have to succeed, but we always have time to set our goals and to start our clocks. To quote Dr. Benjamin E. Mays at Morehouse, *"The tragedy of life does not lie in not reaching your goals. The tragedy lies in having no goals to reach for."*

Dreams have to start somewhere and sometime. The CEO of SELF has to decide how and when.

Twenty Thousand Dollars

When my boss at the Department of the Navy finally told me that my promotion had been delayed each year because I lacked a graduate degree, I decided to earn a master's degree before I was thirty years old. I was twenty-three when I made that decision, and it was, in a sense, not an easy one to make. College had been hard for me, and, on graduating, I left with a pledge to myself—never to set foot in another classroom again. But, when I thought about it, my dream of making $20,000 a year was clearly far more important than staying out of the classroom forever.

So I set some goals: selecting a graduate school, getting admitted to a graduate school, going to graduate school, and graduating with a master's degree.

I decided to get a degree in computer science because it was one of the fastest growing professions in government and business in the 1960's and 1970's. A fast growing profession meant a lot of career and job opportunities, and, presumably, a lot of compensation. Remember, I still had this "make a lot of money" thing in my head.

Purdue University was one of the schools I applied to because I had read somewhere that it was one of the top five (also most difficult) computer science schools in the country. Even though I had found college work difficult, I was determined to attend a top graduate school, because I had not only learned that I needed a master's degree, but that it needed to be from a school with a well-respected reputation. I did not want to do all that work to get a master's degree and then be told later in my career that the degree was from a weak school or program.

Although I applied to several graduate computer science programs, the one I really wanted to attend was Purdue's, because my boss didn't think I would get accepted there, and if I did, he did not think I would be able to complete the program. One of its toughest requirements was to maintain a B average (3.0 out of a possible 4.0) throughout all courses.

> **As CEO of SELF, I decided to reject my boss's opinion and advice.**

As CEO of SELF, I decided to reject my boss's opinion and advice. Even though Mr. Johnson, my high school math teacher, was not directly active on my "Board of Directors," I had always remembered what he had told me about having to work a little harder and longer. I did get admitted to Purdue and I did have to *work a little harder, and a little longer.* As a result, I finished the program in twelve months with a 3.4 grade point average, and received my master's degree.

About a year after I returned to my job unit, I was promoted to a GS-13 supervisory mathematician, with an annual salary of $20,001. I had turned my dream into various en-route goals, and accomplished my "decade goal" (earn $20,000 a year) at age twenty-six instead of thirty. I was now four years ahead of schedule.

Stuck in Neutral

When I decided I wanted to become a corporate vice president, I realized I could not get there working for the government. I put myself in position to begin my climb up the corporate ladder by going to work for Coca-Cola, even though the job represented a lateral salary move. Many of my friends thought that leaving a nice, comfortable, and secure position with the government was a very risky move. It was, but I was the CEO of SELF. They could advise. Only I could decide. And my decision, it turns out, was the right one.

> **Many of my friends thought that leaving a nice, comfortable, and secure position with the government was a very risky move. It was, but only I could decide.**

When Bob Copper decided to ask his boss to create a new position after meeting me, one of the reasons he did so, I later learned, was that I had gotten my master's degree from Purdue. Bob was from Indiana and he knew first-hand of Purdue's outstanding and well-deserved reputation.

After nearly four years of working at Coca-Cola in Atlanta, I started to suspect that a vice presidency was not in my future there. I enjoyed the company and worked on some great projects, but I felt like I was "stuck in neutral." When things are not moving in the right direction, the CEO of SELF has to make the necessary changes. I knew I had to make some changes, because I observed how Coke's then-current vice presidents had ascended to such prestigious levels in the company.

Many were the operating vice presidents—those who had profit and loss responsibility—and most had been with the company a long time. They had worked in fountain sales or marketing, or they had been recruited from outside of the company at a very high level. Staff vice presidents had also been with the company a long time, but there were only a limited number of VP positions for functional areas, such as finance, strategic planning, market research, business analysis, research and development, or information technology.

Operating VPs had usually worked their way up the organization, "paid their dues" by working in the trenches, and "earned their stripes" by consistently delivering bottom-line P & L results. At the time, I had no idea how important it was to work in the trenches of a business before you would even be considered a candidate to run a major segment of the company. There are certainly exceptions, but the road that begins in the trenches is most often the norm.

If I wanted a chance at becoming a vice president at The Coca-Cola Company, I could remain with the company for a long time, get a position in fountain sales or marketing, and *then* work my way up, or I could go to another company. I chose to go to another company, because just as there were low expectations of the "chauffeur's son" prior to the interview with Bob Copper, my suspicion was that the same attitude would persist during my climb at Coca-Cola, no matter how well I performed or how determined I was as CEO of SELF.

The other reason I chose to leave Coca-Cola was its very successful, well-structured, and conservative culture. There was no evidence that such a culture would lend itself to eventually promoting an unlikely candidate like me to vice-president. In fact, I would realize later in my career that the more uncertainty there is in a situation, the more often an unlikely candidate will be considered to handle it.

Vice President

Sensing limited opportunity at Coca-Cola, I happened to read an article on the front page of the *Wall Street Journal* about Bill Spoor, the chairman and CEO of The Pillsbury Company (TPC). Spoor boldly stated that in five years TPC would grow from $1.5 billion in revenue to $5.0 billion. This objective seemed extremely aggressive to me, since it had taken the company 107 years to get to its then-current sales level. Even without knowing how he was going to turn this dream into reality, I could envision the potential opportunities presented, and problems caused, by such a rapid growth rate.

> **The more uncertainty there is in a situation, the more often an unlikely candidate will be considered to handle it.**

Ironically, Bob Copper resigned from Coca-Cola about two weeks later and joined Pillsbury. I thought to myself that Bob either had impeccable timing, or he was just one smart dude. A few months later, Bob made me an offer to join his group at Pillsbury. I chose to join Pillsbury to put myself in a better position to get to corporate vice president, since I had already concluded from reading the *Wall Street Journal* article that my chances might be better there than at Coca-Cola.

When I joined Pillsbury, I was thirty-two years of age. My next "decade goal" was to reach vice-president by the time I turned forty. I was not sure if it was going to happen at Pillsbury, but at least I would be in a better position if I was there. I chose forty as my objective because forty-five was a typical age of corporate vice presidents, and I had hoped I would at least be within shouting distance of that lofty perch by the time I was forty. And, if I were not close by that time, I would have to consider changing my deadline. But, as CEO of SELF, I *never* considered changing the dream itself.

> **I long ago realized that by setting and achieving a decade goal, the "biological clock blues" experienced on reaching thirty, forty, or fifty would not be such a big deal for me.**

The concept of having "decade goals" for each decade of my life seemed very logical to me. It started when I needed to get a master's degree, and I continue the practice even to this day. I long ago realized that by setting and achieving a decade goal, the "biological clock blues" experienced on reaching thirty, forty, or fifty would not be such a big deal for me. I'm not sixty yet, but I'll let you know what happens when I get there.

My hunch about Pillsbury was right. Bob Copper had hired me to help him establish the corporate business analysis function as a well-respected decision support entity within the company. We did just that, and in the process I learned a lot, and gained a lot of exposure to many of the senior executives in the company. Pillsbury's rapid growth generated many great projects for the Business Analysis function in such areas as strategic planning, acquisitions analysis, marketing analysis, operations analysis, and information systems. We were so successful that Bob was promoted to head the much larger MIS (Management Information Systems) department in the Consumer Products Division. I was then promoted to director of the Business Analysis Department.

About eighteen months later, Bob was promoted to vice president of strategic planning for Pillsbury, and I, in turn, was moved up to head the MIS department. Bob and I shared the same dream of becoming a corporate vice president someday, and we also shared a lot of the same CEO of SELF characteristics. We had also become good friends, and next to members of his own family, I was his biggest fan as he made his climb to VP, and even more so when he got there.

As head of the MIS department, I was reporting directly to the president of the Consumer Products Division, and reporting functionally to the corporate vice president of systems, John Haaland. My biggest leadership and technical test came when Pillsbury acquired the Green Giant Company. I was responsible for integrating its MIS Department into the Consumer Products Division's MIS Department. There was obviously a lot of redundancy in systems and positions that had to be eliminated without disrupting the services to the businesses. Many executives, including the chairman and CEO, Bill Spoor, were nervous that if we did not execute the integration smoothly, we could shut down the day-to-day operations of the largest and most profitable division of the company. Gulp!

The integration went as smooth as silk. Less than a year later, John Haaland called me to let me know that he was resigning to pursue *his* dream, and that I had been selected to replace him as corporate vice president of systems. It also happened that the Pillsbury World Headquarters Project was behind schedule and over budget, and Administrative Services needed a home, so John recommended that those functions report to me as well. Bill Spoor agreed, and I was appointed to be the newly titled vice president of systems *and services.*

> **Putting yourself in position to turn your dreams into goals is not an easy thing to do as CEO of SELF, because it may require a major change in your life.**

Putting yourself in position to turn your dreams into goals is not an easy thing to do as CEO of SELF, because it may require a major change in your life or career, or the timing may not.be right. With both the move to Coca-Cola and the move to Pillsbury, I was very fortunate to have had the total support of my wife and vice chairman, Gloria. Without her support, there could easily have been some distracting doubts along the way, which would have made the tough times ahead even tougher. I went to Pillsbury in hopes that its rapid growth would generate rapid opportunities for promotions, and it did. As CEO of SELF, I had to turn those opportunities into stepping-stones by performing outstandingly.

When Pillsbury appointed me vice president, I was thirty-four years old, which was six years earlier than I had dreamed. My biggest challenges in the job were to get approval from the Pillsbury Board of Directors for a new multi-million dollar computer facility, get it built, get the new computer installed, and get all the systems running smoothly. We met all those challenges.

Simultaneously, I was responsible for leading the completion of the Pillsbury World Headquarters Project. This was a decision-making, coordination, communications, and logistical nightmare. I asked the previous executive of the project, who was retiring, to call a meeting to introduce me to everyone responsible for various pieces of the project. I walked into the meeting room, only to find twenty people sitting around a large table. There was a chief attorney, chief engineer, chief architect, chief space planner, chief contractor, chief construction consultant, chief accountant, chief moving manager, and all of their co-chiefs! They looked at me as if to say, "So how are you going to straighten this mess out?" At that moment, I had no idea, because I had not yet talked with each chief to identify the right problems. This was just a get-acquainted session.

My previous boss, John Haaland, knew that the new computer project was well planned and well staffed, and, because it was moving along smoothly, would require very little of my time. But he also knew that the World Headquarters Project was a mess, and would require all of my time, and more.

I knew the dictionary definition of "focus," but I first experienced the concept with the World Headquarters Project, because there was no way I could be concerned with every detail. So, I concentrated on identifying the critical things I needed to get done in order to get the project moving. As you would expect, each "chief" had a different idea of what those critical things were. That's why they needed me.

All of the chiefs were very competent, and as they all pointed out in our one-on-one meetings, our biggest problem was the reluctance of the project's previous executive to make decisions without the approval of Bill Spoor, the chairman and CEO. The previous executive did not see himself as the project's CEO, and so he did not "take charge" of the project to keep it moving. He felt more comfortable deferring to Bill Spoor for most decisions. For him, it was obviously safer to operate that way.

> **Many people fall into a comfort zone of letting other people on their board make decisions for them.**

This happens to many people as CEO of SELF. They fall into a comfort zone of letting other people on their board make decisions for them, because they think it will make the board member happy, or because they want to avoid the risk of being wrong. In either case, they soon lose control of their journey, and ultimately of their dreams.

After a series of meetings with Bill Spoor, Win Wallin (the president and chief operating officer), and all of the division presidents, I developed an overall sense of what they expected and what was most important to them. With their input, I was not afraid to take charge and make decisions. In a sense, I used the chiefs as the project's board of directors, but I had to be its CEO or it would never have gotten completed. I did provide periodic project updates to Bill and Win, and not once did either of them ask me who had decided the carpet color for the thirty-first floor, or other such matters. But I made sure that my chief office designer had Bill's and Win's individual approval before proceeding on their respective office decor.

The World Headquarters Project was completed ahead of schedule and below budget. Two years later, I was presented a Symbol of Excellence in Leadership Award by The Pillsbury Company. Mr. Spoor himself made the presentation.

It took about two years to complete the new computer facility, and to complete the World Headquarters Project. Things were now running so smoothly that I started to get bored. Not only had I achieved my dream of becoming a vice president ahead of schedule, but I had made the most of my opportunity—I had demonstrated that I could get the job done in the position. I needed a new dream.

> **Things were now running so smoothly that I started to get bored. I needed a new dream.**

Vice President Again!

One day while in my office on the thirty-first floor of the Pillsbury World Headquarters building, I started to reflect on what I had enjoyed the most over the previous two years. It was the excitement of making decisions that made things happen. CEOs do that all the time, and so do CEOs of SELF if they want to be happy.

I also started to imagine the excitement of being in charge of a business, instead of being in charge of a project or large functional area. I knew that I was not afraid to be in charge, nor was I afraid to take charge when I had to do so. I also thought about my Dad's failing health and how, starting from nowhere, he had touched so many lives in a positive way. I started to imagine the "chauffeur's son" as president of something. I said the word out loud, and my new dream was born.

Once again, though, I had to put myself in position to turn that dream into goals. Once again, most of my friends thought I was nuts. And once again my vice chairman of SELF, Inc., Gloria, was totally supportive. This led to the bumpy Burger King fast track program, which led to the position as Philadelphia Region vice president and general manager. I had now gotten back to the VP level, at age thirty-seven this time, and was now in position to reach my latest goal—becoming president of something by age fifty. This was a typical age for company presidents, and I had a whole new business to learn and experience—the restaurant business.

The three and a half years at the Philadelphia Region proved every bit as challenging and exciting as I had expected. The newest dimension I had to learn was franchising and working with franchisees. This was a further test of my leadership and persuasive abilities, because many marketing and promotional decisions are made at the discretion of the franchise operator. And even seemingly non-negotiable operations decisions made at headquarters could sometimes meet with resistance from franchisees, if not communicated properly to them.

My region consistently achieved better and better performance results, which proved to be *the* major stepping-stone to becoming president of Godfather's Pizza, Inc. When the call came, I was very excited, and so was my vice chairman, Gloria. I felt no hesitancy in making the move to Omaha, where Godfather's corporate headquarters were located, because that was where I would live out my dream.

If you do not have a dream, then you will not know if you got there.

If you do not have a dream, then you will not know if you got there.

President and CEO

I took over as president of Godfather's on April 1, 1986 at the age of forty! I was now twenty years *ahead* of plan, and thus was loaded with "frequent dreamer miles." I headed Godfather's for ten years, which included buying the company from Pillsbury, because it did not believe Godfather's could survive (another likely situation for an unlikely candidate). I was also asked to join several corporate boards of Fortune 500 companies, which was an unexpected experience and benefit of becoming president of something. When dreams turn to goals, you sometimes find some unexpected "goal dust."

I did not have a new dream in 1996 when I was asked to become president and CEO of the National Restaurant Association. The Association job seemed like it would be a challenge for a while, and for the two and a half years I was there, it *was* a challenge, and I felt good about our accomplishments.

When I left the Association in 1999, I did formulate a new dream, and so I accepted a position as president and CEO of RetailDNA, a start-up technology solutions company. And though I was very proud of the achievements made during the year and a half I ran RetailDNA, it certainly was not the *right* position yet for me to maximize my new dream.

As this book is being written, my professional endeavors are primarily keynote speaking, writing, and continuing to serve on four major corporate boards. I am sharing my experiences with thousands of people a year, and I absolutely love what I am doing.

My rise up the corporate ladder has been described as "meteoric," because it was so fast. It *was* fast, but many things could have derailed my journey along the way. I was blessed, however, with the willingness to dream, great determination and perseverance, an always-supportive vice chairman and members of my Board of Directors who, when I was young, instilled in me a strong belief in God, and a strong belief in myself as CEO of SELF.

4

We Are All CEOs

An Entrepreneur

Entrepreneur: He who casts aside his assurance of forty-hour weeks, leaves the safe cover of tenure and security . . . and charges across the perilous fields of change and opportunity. If he succeeds, his profits will come not from what he takes from his fellow citizens, but from the value they freely place on the gift of his imagination.

—George Gilder

We Are All CEOs

Many books have identified and analyzed numerous leadership skills and characteristics, but few have left the reader with a day-to-day model of concepts and principles that can be applied spontaneously and repeatedly. Leadership concepts and principles applied spontaneously and repeatedly become *common sense.* The more you use them, the better you will be as CEO of SELF.

It's Common Sense

A CEO is a leader . . . hence the term, chief executive officer. No matter how complicated life gets, self-leadership is still common sense, because the critical characteristics and the critical things a SELF-CEO must do remain unchanged. Great leaders instinctively possess these qualities. Good leaders have to work at them consciously, but they are as fundamental as breathing.

A leader must be *self-motivated*, willing to *take some risks* and then willing to make the tough decisions. And he must have the ability to *block out the unnecessary* "stuff" to be able to concentrate on the necessary.These are the three critical qualities a leader must possess. I call these the D, E, and F factors.

D (Drucker) Ability to recognize that people must motivate themselves

E (Entrepreneurial) Ability to take risks and make the tough decisions

F (Focus) Ability to block out the unnecessary and concentrate on the necessary

> **A leader must be *self-motivated*, willing to *take some risks,* and must have the ability to *block out the unnecessary "stuff."***

There are three critical things a leader must do. I call these the R, O, and I factors.

R (Remove) barriers that prevent people from being self-motivated

O (Obtain) the right results by working on the right problems

I (Inspire) the passion within people to perform better than expected

Three Critical CEO Characteristics

The D-Factor

During my employment with The Coca-Cola Company in the mid 1970s, I had the opportunity to attend a seminar where the well-known "management thinker" Peter Drucker was a speaker. Over the years, I regret to say, I have retained little from the numerous presentations I have attended on the subject of leadership, but I distinctly remember one thing Drucker said during this seminar. His comment about motivation shaped my attitude about self-leadership forever. Drucker said, "You can't motivate people. You can only thwart their motivation because people must motivate themselves."

This principle, which I call the *D-factor* in honor of Drucker, has significantly affected my relationships with people since the day I heard it presented by Drucker. But more importantly, I have experienced its truth over and over again in my own decisions as CEO of SELF. I was self-motivated to make the many changes I made in my career. High self-motivation is not a characteristic that everyone possesses, which is why I consider it one a leader *must* possess. Without it, and without being able to recognize it in other people, one cannot lead anybody anywhere.

> **You can't motivate people. You can only thwart their motivation because people must motivate themselves.**

I did not grow up with the feeling that I was a born leader or that I always had to be the leader. But I have always been results-oriented—with ambition and determination. I do not know how or why some people are more ambitious, determined, or results-oriented than others, but I'm sure there is a research study out there somewhere that has tried to answer that question. My intent is not to advance the "science" of leadership, but to advance the "art" of leadership to help you achieve your success *and* happiness as CEO of SELF.

At each major decision point in my life and career, my own motivation has come from a deep desire to exceed expectations and make a difference. In doing so, I have found much joy in life, and I have experienced the true secret to success—happiness. If you are happy doing what you are doing, then you will be successful. You may not find it in that first job you thought was going to be your last, but remember: "Success is a journey"—and so is happiness.

> **If you are happy doing what you are doing, then you will be successful.**

The biggest challenge you will have as CEO of SELF is determining what really makes you happy. This is not independent of your job or career, and you may not find that happiness in your current job. If you do, you are one of the lucky ones. If you do not, you will have to establish a long-term plan for change. You will naturally be self-motivated every day *if* you are happy doing what you are doing. As I climbed the corporate ladder, I was always self-motivated by my *next* dream, because I was doing something to prepare myself for my next dream. I was also living well—not "large," just well.

The E-Factor

There is a lot of truth to the old saying that the only things certain in life are death and taxes. That means everything else in life is risky. Leadership is especially risky because every time you make a decision, you run the risk of being wrong . . . but you also run the risk of being right!

Different people are comfortable with different levels of risk. Some people will bet all they own on an idea or hunch, while others would not bet one dime of someone else's money on a seemingly sure thing. People select and pursue different careers because of the risks that are often associated with their "risk index." Think of the index as having a range between 1 and 10. The lower the index number, the less risk people are naturally willing to take. If their index is higher, they will take more risk. Successful CEOs of SELF are willing to take some calculated risks to achieve their definition of success and happiness, and they usually have an index of 5 or higher. What is *your* risk index?

> **A leader must be comfortable with risk in order to be able to make decisions.**

A leader must be comfortable with risk in order to be able to make decisions. A leader must also be prepared to be wrong, but good leaders tend to make more correct decisions than incorrect ones. In fact, there really is no such thing as a right or wrong decision, just different consequences for taking different actions. If the consequences are desired, then it was a "right" decision.

No one enjoys the feeling of being *wrong* about anything, but some people dislike being wrong more than others. Consequently, they try to minimize the risk of being wrong by not making a decision at all, or having others impose the decision on them. There is another old saying, "If you can't stand the heat, stay out of the kitchen." Leaders are "in the kitchen" all the time, taking risks. And if you are afraid to be in the kitchen as CEO of SELF, then you will have to settle for Second In Command (SIC), and not be as happy as you could be.

In decision making, the risky part occurs after all the analysis and evaluation on a problem or opportunity have been done, because you must then complete the decision making process based on what's inside of you . . . your "gut feeling." People with a very low risk index are very uncomfortable making "gut calls," due largely to their fear of being wrong. People with a high risk index are not only comfortable making such calls, but they are usually excited about having the responsibility.

> **After making a decision, good leaders work to achieve the desired outcome by using all of their creative energies and instincts to overcome obstacles along the way.**

After making a decision, good leaders work to achieve the desired outcome by using all of their creative energies and instincts to overcome obstacles along the way. If they are wrong, they are self-motivated enough (*D-factor*) to reevaluate, regroup, learn from the experience, and go on.

The entrepreneurial spirit (*E-factor*) in a person is not a reckless abandonment of logic or common sense. It is an intuitive and positive view of the world as "a glass half full" instead of "a glass half empty." Success and happiness cannot be achieved without some risks, or without a dream.

The entrepreneurial characteristic found in good leaders allows them to use their creative talents positively to eliminate barriers and obstacles, then to achieve the desired results from decisions made. Dr. Robert Schuller, pastor of the Crystal Cathedral Ministries of Garden Grove, California, calls it "possibility thinking." I call it the E-factor.

The F-Factor

My first exposure to the "business-speak" concept of *focus* occurred on my first trip to Omaha, Nebraska. The Pillsbury Company had appointed me president of Godfather's Pizza, Inc. (GPI), effective April 1, 1986. But long before being appointed GPI president, I had made plans to attend the NCAA Final Four basketball tournament in Dallas, Texas, which happened to fall on the weekend immediately before my first day on the new job.

I decided to go anyway. En route from Philadelphia to Dallas, I found a book in the overhead compartment in which I quickly became engrossed. Entitled *Marketing Warfare*, written by Al Ries and Jack Trout, it was so absorbing I continued to read it until we landed in Dallas. While in Dallas, I remained so hooked that before I boarded my flight to Omaha that Tuesday morning, April 1, I had finished the book.

In *Marketing Warfare*, Ries and Trout discuss the concept of defensive marketing strategy when you are not the first, second, or even the third largest competitor in a market. The first principle of this concept is to focus your resources, because a smaller competitor cannot afford to fight a larger competitor on his larger turf or on his expansive terms. As I was reading *Marketing Warfare*, I was continually thinking of GPI because my boss, Jeff Campbell, had clearly described what I would be facing at GPI as its new president.

Although I have always been a cut-to-the-chase, get-to–the-heart, what's-the-bottom-line, kind of person, this was the first time I had ever read anything that discussed the concept of focus so explicitly. It had an especially strong impact on me because I was on my way to take over a company in decline. I had some ideas about how I would approach the situation because Jeff had asked me to put together a hundred-day plan of attack, site unseen. But when I found the book, I found the theme of what we needed to do to turn GPI around . . . I found *focus*.

> "The essence of focus is sacrifice." Leaders who cannot bring themselves to give up the unnecessary "stuff" for the sake of the necessary do not possess the critical leadership characteristic of focus.

Becoming president of a business was a dream of mine on which I never lost my focus, so when it came along, I did not have to hesitate.

The ability to block out the unnecessary "stuff" is the willingness to concentrate your resources for more impact, just as one can deliver a more forceful blow with a fist than with an open palm. But as Ries and Trout point out, "The essence of focus is sacrifice." Leaders who cannot bring themselves to give up the unnecessary "stuff" for the sake of the necessary do not possess the critical leadership characteristic of focus.

In order to enhance your shareholders' value in SELF, Inc., you might have to give up some things to be more effective overall. In order to pursue a master's degree, which was so important to my career, I had to give up the hope of never again having to set foot in a classroom as a student.

> **Establishing focus as CEO of SELF requires a willingness to make the necessary decisions.**

Establishing focus as a leader is not just a matter of using the word. It is also a matter of actions and convictions. Establishing focus as CEO of SELF requires a willingness to make the necessary decisions. Just like that old Negro spiritual says, "Everybody talking about heaven ain't going there," not everyone who can spell "focus" will know how to focus themselves or their organization.

People who know me know that I am a Christian believer. I believe God wanted me to find that book when I did . . . because He wanted me to succeed at GPI. To the person who bought the book *Marketing Warfare* and left it on an airplane. . . thank you!

Three Critical Things a CEO Must Do

The R Factor

The list of barriers to self-motivation is endless, but the most common obstacles can be classified as job-related, family-related, or personal—all of which can adversely affect a person's success, happiness, and sense of CEO of SELF.

It is the leader's direct responsibility to identify and *remove* job-related barriers, such as:

- ► putting or keeping someone in the wrong job;
- ► poor communication;
- ► inadequate training;
- ► improper working facilities;
- ► and other barriers shown on page 73.

These are barriers that can keep individuals from maintaining focus on the job and performing their best.

At the top of the previous list of job-related barriers (although they are not arranged in order of importance) is "wrong job." This potential barrier is the most difficult to deal with. If you, for any reason, are in the wrong job, removing the barrier requires time and a plan. For some people, it means getting another job. But this is not an easy thing to do because of the security the current job may provide.

For those who are nearing retirement, fear of the unknown, or uncertainty about it, may dictate hanging in there until they retire. But if you must "hang in there" because you have been there so long, at least begin to set some goals for retirement, and start the clock. This time, make sure those goals will make you happy.

Barriers

Job-related:

Wrong job	Discrimination
Poor communications	Feeling unappreciated
Job insecurity (fear)	Feeling of entitlement
Poor performance	Feeling underpaid
Low challenge (too easy)	Personality conflict
Second job	Inadequate Training

Personal:

Not "happy"	Inflated ego
Low risk index	Lazy
Low self-confidence	Dull person
Low self-esteem	Bad attitude

Family-related:

Miserable marriage	Death of a loved one
Too much debt	Divorce
Problem child	No family
Problem relative	Illness

If you are unhappy in your job early in your career or in mid-career, your decision is a lot tougher. Your E-factor kicks in if you have found another opportunity that puts you in a position to move toward your dream job. Making a job change is always a risk, because there is no such thing as a sure thing. I advise my now grown kids, as they start their working careers, *never to quit a job until they have another job . . . Don't be stupid just because you are unhappy.* But it is your decision to make as CEO of SELF.

Some people have experienced the joy of being in the *right* job, which usually makes most of the other job-related barriers irrelevant. When you are in the right job, you will often find ways to resolve job-related barriers, and in some instances you can and will just ignore petty barriers because you are too busy enjoying your job. The more people complain about petty stuff in their job, the more they should find a "new road" to somewhere else.

Win Wallin is one of my leadership heroes. Although he may never be a household name, Win Wallin is a great American business leader. Win was president and COO (chief operating officer) of The Pillsbury Company when I started there in 1977, and he's the one who suggested that I go to work for Burger King if I ever wanted to be president of something.

Win's career at Pillsbury under Bill Spoor (chairman and CEO) was impressive—nearly twenty successive years of compound earnings growth. Even more impressive was Win's record at Medtronic, Incorporated, where he became chairman and CEO. From 1985 through 1995, Medtronic sales posted a compound annual growth rate of 16.7 percent, and a compound annual growth in net earnings of 22.7 percent. Earnings per share grew 24.3 percent, with a ten-year average return on equity of 21.6 percent. Not bad for someone the Pillsbury Board of Directors did not feel was the right guy to succeed Bill Spoor as chairman and CEO on his retirement. History has indeed shown that Win was the right person for the right job . . . CEO at Medtronic, Inc.

When I asked Win for his views on leadership, he responded in typical Win Wallin fashion, "I've really not thought much about it." But a moment later, he singled out as most significant "Identifying good people with talent and putting them in positions they enjoy." I did not know at the time that I would later call Win an inspired CEO of SELF. But this is an example of Win Wallin's instinctive leadership qualities, which makes him a great leader in my book.

> **When I asked Win Wallin for his views on leadership, he responded, "Identifying good people with talent and putting them in positions they enjoy."**

When he first suggested that I should give up my comfortable vice-president's job and go to work for Burger King, starting at the bottom, I wondered for a moment if Win was trying to get rid of me. But he must have seen something in me that I did not realize, because it was some of the best advice I have ever received. I am glad I acted on it. I have been a vice president of Burger King, president of Godfather's Pizza, Inc., CEO of the National Restaurant Association, CEO of a start-up technology solutions company, and today CEO of T.H.E. Inc, which is my own leadership consulting business. Is this a great country or what? It all started with that first dream and giving myself permission to be CEO of SELF.

Family-related barriers are generally more difficult to remove than personal or job-related ones. That's no surprise—you cannot change who you have for parents, siblings, or children. You can ignore friends and acquaintances, but not the uncle who embarrasses everybody at the family reunion. And of course, your children are yours for life. A child gone wrong can be a constant distraction to one's personal and professional focus, making it an awesome barrier to overcome.

Family and personal problems are barriers to self-motivation both at home and in the workplace. They are always stressful and difficult to handle, but ultimately their resolution is *your* responsibility. Although many family problems can be handled through improved communication, it is sometimes necessary to get outside professional help. If this is the case, don't hesitate too long in getting it.

> **When barriers are removed, people are happier.**

When barriers are removed, people are happier. The fewer the barriers, the happier they are. People usually remain happy until they start focusing on another barrier instead of their dream. But identifying and removing barriers is habit forming, which makes solving problems a habit as well, and before you know it, happiness is a habit. When you get in the habit of being happy, you are in the habit of being in charge as CEO of SELF.

The O Factor
The first critical step in *obtaining the right result* is to determine if you are working on the right problem. This requires asking the right questions. Although this may seem obvious, it is too often overlooked, taken for granted, or misidentified.

During my first sixty days at Godfather's Pizza, I asked the director of human resources when we had last conducted HR audits in our restaurants. An HR audit simply verifies that all legally required notices are posted properly and that documentation on each restaurant employee is, in fact, available and current. If these things had not been done, we would have been subject to fines by the U.S. Department of Labor. Since we were trying to achieve profitability again, the last thing I wanted to spend money on were federal fines. We needed every dime we could find to rebuild the business.

The HR director informed me that we had never done HR audits. This admission, made during a meeting of staff members reporting directly to me, caused me to have a conniption fit (some called it a "Cainniption fit"). I directed the HR chief to perform an HR audit immediately on all two hundred company-owned restaurants. I also asked him not to let me see him in Omaha, not even on weekends, until he had finished that task. I imposed focus on him. I excused him from the meeting so he could begin right away. Unsurprisingly, he completed the task in an amazingly short time, after which he returned to staff meetings and his other HR duties.

More often than not, asking yourself or others the right question avoids "developing a new mouse trap" when all that's needed is to better utilize the one you have. Asking the right questions produces more of the right decisions.

It is possible, however, to make the right decision and still not achieve the desired result due to poor execution and weak management of the details, in which case, you have another question to ask . . . do you have the right people?

In my example, the right question to the HR director was, "When was the last time we performed HR audits in our company restaurants?" The wrong answer was, "What's an HR audit?"

In deciding whether to leave my comfortable corporate VP job at Pillsbury to start over at Burger King, the right question was, "Will this put me in a better position to become president of a business?" I did not ask myself how hard the new job would be, what my friends would think if they saw me making hamburgers in a quick service restaurant, or what I would do if this new position did not work out as planned. These last three questions were not the right questions for a CEO of SELF. I was focused on my dream.

> **If the right questions are not asked, then the real problems—the biggest problems—will go unsolved.**

Some decisions can be made in more than one way, or they can be subdivided into incremental decisions. Either way, the process begins with asking the right questions. If the right questions are not asked, then the real problems—the biggest problems—will go unsolved.

Developing and selecting the right alternative solution to a problem or opportunity can range from a "no-brainer" to a very complicated analysis. But the person or persons closest to the situation can usually provide the best ideas and alternatives on where to start. By the same token, the person closest to CEO of SELF is you!

Sometimes, though, even the most well-analyzed and best-planned decision can still run into speed bumps. When this happens, the CEO and leader must keep things on track and on time by effectively dealing with obstacles, or making sure someone has the delegated authority to do so. When progress is stalled by indecisiveness, procrastination, or not enough E-factor, a leader must lead. A leader must initiate action, and then follow-up until things are running smoothly toward the desired results.

Are you asking the right questions about SELF, Inc., and are you asking yourself the hard questions? Leadership of SELF begins with being honest with SELF. It is a step no one can take for you, except you.

CEOs look, listen, learn, and then lead.

> **Leadership of SELF begins with being honest with SELF. It is a step no one can take for you, except you.**

The I Factor

The *American Heritage Dictionary* defines *inspire* this way: "To stimulate to creativity or action." In your case, I hope it is positive creativity or positive action. A person's determination or self-motivation can be inspired to a higher level. A person's belief in something can be inspired. His inner energy can be inspired. His faith can be inspired. Inspiration is self-motivation plus passion about something in which you believe strongly.

CEOs of SELF are inspired by their dream. A leader's ability to inspire others is determined by his ability to demonstrate self-motivation and passion. This is why what a leader says and what a leader does are so important. A leader's credibility while attempting to inspire the troops is most often enhanced by the leader's past accomplishments, his or her formal credentials, a shared belief or point of view, personal characteristics such as a reputation for high integrity, and D-E-F leadership characteristics or charisma (personal magnetism or charm). When leading yourself, what works is something called self-confidence. No one has ever achieved his dreams without confidence in himself.

> **No one has ever achieved his dreams without confidence in himself.**

When I came to Godfather's Pizza and boldly stated in my opening speech that GPI could succeed, I was believed because the audience knew I had taken a poorly performing Burger King region and turned it around (which was one of the reasons I was selected to become president of Godfather's Pizza). In fact, my entire career had been deemed a "meteoric" rise in the corporate world. So why not believe this guy when he said the company could win again?

Most people like to win. They like to be on a winning team or to be a part of a winning effort. The desire to win inspires people. A leader who projects a winning attitude or winning ways attracts people who also want to win. When you project this winning attitude as CEO of SELF, your Board of Directors *will* be more supportive. They might still whine at times, but they will be more supportive.

If done appropriately, actions can inspire as well as words. It is inspiring when the leader just rolls up his sleeves with the people. I have walked into some of my restaurants when the unit was getting "slammed." Instead of yelling at the manager, I would start cleaning off tables if they needed it, or assist a cashier to help speed things up. No one can roll up your sleeves for your success and happiness *except you*.

Another example of actions inspiring other people was when I appeared on a nationally televised town hall meeting and challenged then-President Clinton on the flaws in his proposed health care plan. Afterward, many people wrote or called me expressing their happiness that I had asked the president the "right question."

Many people went on to comment that my example had *inspired* them to write or call their own senators or congressional representatives because they shared my views that his health care plan would have a negative impact on jobs. The restaurant industry had become mobilized against the plan because of the disproportionately large number of entry-level and first-time workers hired by our industry, and the relatively high employee turnover rate. I never expected that one event to inspire so many people to speak up and to speak out.

When I had my "Cainniption fit" about the lack of HR audits, my actions sent a message about the importance of being in compliance with appropriate legal requirements. The outburst inspired other departments to assess their compliance activities to avoid a similar "Cainniption."

Now, I am not suggesting that this will work for everyone—of course it will not. It worked for me because of my personality and my leadership style. I tried to do it so that the HR director understood my view that the problem was serious, but that the target of my "Cainniption" was not the HR director himself.

The first GPI system-wide speech I gave in 1986 inspired people to believe in Godfather's Pizza's opportunity to be successful again. Although some of the people who heard that speech already shared my belief about the potential for our success, even more of the audience became inspired because they were convinced that I believed what I was saying, which I did. As we began to successfully implement some of the ideas we had developed and to achieve some of our goals, the credibility of that opening speech, and my credibility as the leader, were enhanced.

> **The leader who pooh-poohs the value of being able to inspire his people through the spoken word will miss many opportunities to enhance performance, productivity, and creativity.**

The leader who pooh-poohs the value of being able to inspire his people through the spoken word will miss many opportunities to enhance performance, productivity, and creativity. Obviously, not everyone is born a great speaker, but most people can become good speakers if they work at it (read my earlier book, *Speak As A Leader*, if you want to improve your speaking skills). Words are like music. They can touch the heart and soul if they are the right words spoken the right way at the right time . . . and you can deliver on what you say.

As CEO of SELF, you must talk to yourself as well. You may not want to do it in public, but you cannot always wait for the right inspiring words from someone else when you need them. You must begin by saying your dreams out loud.

We are all leaders of SELF. Leaders take people to where they would not go by themselves. The CEO of SELF is the only one who can take you to where your dreams are. The great philosopher Socrates said, "Know thyself." "The Hermanator" says, "Inspire thyself" and "Talk to thyself."

5

You're in Charge

Freedom

No man is free who is not master of himself.
—Epictetus

You're in Charge

Be Happy First

You are the CEO of SELF, Inc. You not only deserve to be happy, but it is your *responsibility* to be happy. If the CEO is not happy, then shareholder value cannot be maximized, because *happiness is the key to success.*

If you do not already have one, your first responsibility is to establish a dream (vision) for SELF, Inc. Your dream can include the dreams or goals of your major stockholders (immediate family), but do not confuse satisfying their needs and desires with your dreams. One of your goals may be helping your spouse achieve something he or she is working to accomplish, or it may be seeing your children graduate from technical school or college. But your dreams should look beyond their goals, because one day those goals will be mere destination points in your rearview mirror.

Your dream does not have to be spectacular, but it does have to be *your* dream. In the same sense that Drucker observed that "You cannot motivate people," no one else can make you happy. You must make yourself happy, and it starts with your dream. When that dream becomes a destination point in your rearview mirror, get another dream, but be happy first as CEO of SELF.

The Happiness Equation

Your dream as CEO of SELF is one-third of the happiness equation:

- ➤ Something to do,
- ➤ Someone to love, and
- ➤ Something to hope for.

Most people have something to do, even if it is not what they prefer to do. Most people also have someone to love, even if it is only their pet. With most unhappy people, the missing component is the dream, the absence of *something to hope for*. But, if any component of the happiness equation is missing in your life, then you are, most likely, not happy.

> **With most unhappy people, the missing component is the dream, the absence of *something to hope for*.**

Something to do means either work or play. Whether they like it or not, work is necessary for most people in order to have the necessary resources (money) to satisfy their needs and desires. Only a few people are fortunate enough to be working at something they really love. If you are one of the lucky few, then thank your lucky stars every day. If you are not one of the lucky ones who love their job, then maybe that could become one of your dreams. But, you need a plan.

And remember the advice I gave to my two adult children, *"Don't be stupid just because you are unhappy. Find a new job before quitting your current one."* Your dream can be postponed until the timing is appropriate, but don't give up on your dream, and don't just "settle." As CEO of SELF, you must, first and foremost, give yourself permission to dream.

> **Don't be stupid just because you are unhappy.**

As a senior math major at Morehouse College, I was thrilled when the department head asked me to teach one of the freshman math classes. They even paid me to do this part-time job, and I definitely needed the money. It wasn't much back then, because somehow even minimum wage did not apply to teaching assistants.

I absolutely loved teaching math those two semesters, but my dream was to draw $20,000 in annual salary long before I turned sixty-five years old. Teaching has never been near the top of the income chart, even though it is near the top of the value to humanity chart. My dream included being at the top of both charts.

Today, schedule permitting, I still get to speak at colleges and universities, and each time I give one of these guest lectures, I am inspired by the student feedback I receive. Some students simply tell me they really got a lot out of my talk, and others, with tears in their eyes, will thank me for helping to open their eyes.

Most people consider what they really enjoy doing as play, and they're right, because if they do not enjoy doing it, then it is nothing more than work. And, if you do not enjoy doing something and, worse still, it is not helping you as CRG (chief revenue generator) for SELF, Inc., why do it?

One of my "play" interests is music, and I have even recorded a gospel CD as a vocalist. I did not choose music as a profession, because no matter how talented I might be, being a professional singer entails too much risk and too much financial uncertainty.

> **Most people consider what they really enjoy doing as play, and they're right, because if they do not enjoy doing it, then it is nothing more than work.**

And, just as only a few people love their job, even fewer people have been able to turn their "play" into "work" with enough pay to satisfy their needs and desires. Music has always been very satisfying to me for relaxation and play, but I chose not to rely on music for my work and pay.

The second component of the happiness equation is having *someone to love*, because everybody wants some love in their life. It is a basic need. This idea is consistent with the theory of the famous psychologist Abraham Maslow, who believed that people are motivated to satisfy unmet needs. As one level of need is satisfied, said Maslow, people are then motivated to satisfy the next level. The chart below shows that the need for love or belonging is second only to satisfying such basic human needs as food and shelter, and the need to be safe and to feel safe.

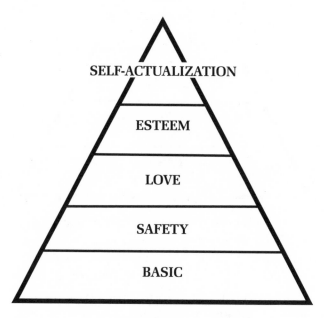

Maslow's Hierarchy of Needs

The importance of *someone to love* was also underscored by Kennon M. Sheldon in a more recent study, which appeared in the *Journal of Personality and Social Psychology*. Sheldon's research identified "relatedness" (belonging) as one of the top four human needs—the other three were autonomy, competence, and self-esteem—for people to be happy.

His findings were consistent across different age groups, time periods, and cultures. They were also consistent with Maslow's hierarchy, because it is logical that the need to feel "competent" allows people to satisfy their "basic" needs and "safety" needs.

Maslow's Needs/Sheldon's Psychological Needs

Loved ones fill a critical need for your happiness, which is why they are on your Board of Directors, where they provide you something of varying value. Most of them offer valuable advice, but we all have some relatives who are more trouble than help.

Another psychologist, Stephen Reiss of Ohio State University, writing in the publication *Psychology Today*, says happiness is determined by "satisfying the five or six desires that are most important to you." His list includes sixteen basic desires which are also on Maslow's Hierarchy and Sheldon's top four, but he says that different people prioritize their five or six key desires differently in order to be happy, which is what makes us individuals. This also suggests that people prioritize dreams differently, which is why *a dream must be your dream*. The dreams of your loved ones are important, the vision of your business or the company you work for is also important, but the dream must be for SELF, Inc.

Reiss also makes the distinction between two kinds of happiness. "Feel-good" happiness is sensation-motivated pleasure, such as laughter, sex, eating, or drinking alcohol. "Value-based" happiness is purpose-motivated, which is a sense that our lives have meaning and fulfill some larger purpose. Reiss states, "Feel-good happiness is ruled by the law of diminishing returns, because the kicks get harder to come by. Whereas, value-based happiness is ruled by the law of increasing returns, because there is no limit to how meaningful our lives can be."

> **Something to hope for is the most critical component of the happiness equation.**

This is why, in my experience, *something to hope for* is the most critical component of the happiness equation. When I gave myself permission to dream of making $20,000 a year, I was motivated, in part, by the desire to acquire the means necessary to experience some of life's pleasures. Once acquired, I kept "raising the bar," but along the way I made the lives of my primary stockholders better, and I made the lives better for the people associated with the businesses I helped to make successful. I felt good about achieving my dreams, but the real value was the impact my success had on other people.

Maslow, Kennon, and Reiss validate all or part of the happiness equation, and, if you eliminate their slight differences in wording, they essentially arrive at the same conclusions. The happiness equation, on the other hand, gives you a day-to-day working model to use as CEO of SELF.

Evaluate the components of *your* happiness equation. Ask yourself the hard questions about each component, then look in the mirror and answer yourself. If you like the answers, you will be smiling at yourself when you finish. If you do not like the answers you get when you add them up, then you may have to *remove some barriers* in order to be *happier*. It's your choice as CEO of SELF.

Something to do, someone to love, and something to hope for, the greatest of these is *hope.*

> *Something to do, someone to love, and something to hope for,* **the greatest of these is** *hope.*

Love You, Mom, But I Gotta Go

At some point in everyone's life you must decide to be CEO of SELF, or to remain Second In Command (SIC, pronounced "sick") forever. We are all born SIC as human beings, totally dependent on other human beings for our survival early in life. As we grow and mature we become more and more self-sufficient and independent. For some people finishing their formal education from high school or college marks the beginning of stepping out on their own. For others, early independence is forced due to circumstances beyond their control. In both instances, events and life changing decisions can begin to compound and cause people to slip into second place in their own lives.

There are three primary life-changing events that can cause CEO of SELF slippage: Mom and Dad trying to hold on when you tell them you love them but to let go, marriage, and having children. Each of these major events requires some compromise, but compromising to the point of forgetting your dreams and being SIC of SELF will make you very unhappy.

When I graduated from Morehouse College in 1967 and accepted a job with the Department of the Navy, I had to move to the small town of Dahlgren, Virginia. My mother did not understand why I could not just get a job in Atlanta, because I now had, as she put it, "all that education."

Dad was much more understanding of my need to leave. Eventually, with a mother's love, Mom accepted my leaving, but it would be years before she would really appreciate why I had to leave her home city to pursue a career. When I moved back to Atlanta early in my career to work for The Coca-Cola Company, Mom could not have been happier. I had a good job with The Coca-Cola Company and my family and I were back living in Atlanta. Mom could now enjoy both of her granddaughters, Melanie and Adrienne (Thurman's first daughter) without having to travel a long distance.

When I later informed her that I had accepted a job with Pillsbury, and that we were going to move to Minneapolis, the conflict of dreams started all over again. "Why," she asked, "do you want to go all the way to Minneapolis when you have a good job here at The Coca-Cola Company?" Once again, Dad understood, because I had shared with him my dream of becoming a corporate vice president, and he agreed with me—and with my reasoning—that a VP was probably not in my future at Coca-Cola.

When my name first appeared in *Ebony Magazine* (it was a profile of me as a vice president of The Pillsbury Company) Mom proudly showed the article to everyone she knew, and nearly everyone she did not know. Later, when I became president of Godfather's Pizza, Inc., and CEO of the National Restaurant Association, Mom loved seeing and reading the many articles about me and my companies that appeared in newspapers and industry publications. Her pride was obvious.

One day not long after Dad's death, when just the two of us were talking, she told me how proud she was of me and that I had really done well. I told her that's why I'd had to leave home after college in that raggedy old Mustang to start my career in Dahlgren, Virginia. She just laughed. Later, after I was no longer CEO of those well-known companies and organizations, she asked me what I was doing with myself. I explained that I was now a professional keynote speaker, which meant I got paid for speaking. She was surprised and responded, "You get paid to talk?"

> When you are growing up, your parents are obviously the most important members of your Board of Directors, but there comes a time when you must promote yourself to CEO of SELF.

Though multiple sclerosis has severely limited Mom's physical activity at age seventy-six, her attitude about life remains as positive as ever. She must have gotten that attitude from her mother, who lived to be 104 years old.

When you are growing up, your parents are obviously the most important members of your Board of Directors, but there comes a time when you must promote yourself to CEO of SELF, and sometimes it'll feel as if you're doing so without their vote or their love.

There are, obviously, a few exceptions when going out on your own is not appropriate relative to timing or family conditions. But, that still need not keep you from taking charge of SELF, though it may mean putting your dreams on hold. If you do not promote yourself, you are, as I've stated in this book, "stuck in SIC" (Second-in-Command).

The Marriage Equation

Marriage is probably the biggest decision we ever make, but we only get half the votes. The person you want to marry gets the other half. If the person says yes, then he or she becomes vice chairman of your board of SELF, Inc.

I am not about to give advice on how to have a successful marriage, or why marriages fail. There are plenty of books on that subject. But I am an expert on why I believe Gloria and I have been married successfully for thirty-three years. Gloria might have a different explanation, but mine has to do with love, mutual respect for each other as vice chairmen and CEOs of SELF, and our two happiness equations, which complement each other.

When Gloria and I first met, it was "a little lust" at first sight: I had the "lust" and she wanted "little" to do with me. We were introduced by a mutual friend in front of my father's neighborhood grocery store, on a summer afternoon before an evening party being given by our mutual friend, Ruth. In the fall, I would begin my sopho-more year at Morehouse, and Gloria would be a fresh-man at Morris Brown College.

After an introduction and an exchange of pleasant-ries, we talked briefly until I had to go inside to serve a store customer. But I was excited that I would see her that night at the party. The irony is that Ruth had been telling me for at least two years that she wanted me to meet her "little sister" Gloria, but never having had a good experience with a blind date, I was always "busy."

At the party that night, I tried like there was no tomorrow to talk to Gloria, but she had zero interest in me. It was very obvious, because she spent most of her time talking to someone who was then a student at Mor-ris Brown. Thankfully, it was a she, which spared my ego a little bit.

That night at the party, Gloria's priority as CEO of SELF was learning as much as she could about the new experience she was looking forward to in the fall, not some dude who she thought "talked too much." Though, with my best moves I was trying to inspire her to go out with me, I got nowhere. This was twenty years before I heard of Drucker's principle, *"You can't motivate people. People must motivate themselves."*

She did give me her phone number, however, and I called her nearly every night for two weeks after that, but she just did not have time to go out with me then. While I still had some ego left, I postponed my dream of dating this girl who clearly had priorities that did not include me. During the next year and a half, I would occasionally see Gloria on the campus of Morris Brown when my buddy, Roswell, and I would go over to "check things out." I did not ask her out, but we would chat briefly when I ran into her.

Finally, during the Christmas break of her sopho-
more year and my junior year in college, I called her
and asked her out—and she accepted! We went to a
movie on our first date, and started dating regularly,
and soon it was lust and love for both of us. We became
engaged a year and a half later, after I had graduated
from Morehouse. A year after that, when she had graduated from Morris Brown College, we were married.

Marriage requires some compromises, which you
must be willing to make if you love someone. But,
though Gloria and I made plenty of compromises, we
did not compromise our identities. Like many young
couples, we tried at first to *change* each other, but we
quickly learned that you cannot change a person. You
must learn to accept and respect the differences that
make us individuals, and you must also learn to support each other's goals and dreams.

> **Marriage requires some com-
> promises, which you must be
> willing to make if you love
> someone. But, though Gloria
> and I made plenty of compro-
> mises, we did not compromise
> our identities.**

Before we got married, we talked a lot about our
dreams and our future together. Prior to meeting me,
Gloria's dream was to promote herself to CEO of SELF,
move out of her mother's house, make her own money,
get her own apartment, buy her own car, and be completely on her own. Obviously, autonomy was a big priority for Gloria.

My dream was to be an extremely successful corporate executive who could provide more than comfortably for my family-to-come. I knew my dream would require us to relocate from time to time as I moved up the corporate ladder. As these moves became necessary, it would also mean that Gloria would have to disrupt her career, since I was old-fashioned and wanted to be the primary breadwinner. I promised her that if she was willing to make that compromise, life together would be an adventure! I also told her that even if my grandiose plans for success did not work out, I would dig ditches if I had to in order to feed us and keep a roof over our heads. She never forgot that promise, and our joint adventure goes on.

It helped that we shared the same religious faith, and that we both wanted children, so no compromises were necessary on these two important subjects. But we did have one major disagreement, at least at first. I wanted four children, and told her so. Even though she didn't immediately react, she later told me what she was really thinking—*"No way!"* As it turned out, she was right. Two was actually the right number of children for us.

When two people get married, two equations of happiness are added together. If they match perfectly, which is very rare, you get a marriage bonus, as in "two plus two equals five."

If two people are a good match, their love enables them to reach some compromises, which is good and fine so long as the two individuals do not also have to modify their own identities. In that case, which is the most common, the result is simple addition, as in "two plus two equals four."

If the marriage equation adds up to "two plus two equals three," both spouses lose something by putting their two happiness equations together. At this point, they must evaluate the deficiencies, and identify what needs to be done as two CEOs.

The objective in marriage is to have more days when two plus two adds up to four or five, than days when the tally is three or even two.

Something to do, someone to love, and something to hope for are the three components of happiness.

In marriage, the most important of these is *love.*

Here Come the Kids

The first time you say, "Love you, Mom, but I gotta go," you can experience the feeling of being your own CEO. This includes the slight fear that comes from knowing you must totally support yourself. You gotta eat, and it's all up to you. But at least, as a single person, you do not have to make many compromises other than lifestyle (and these are mostly based on your income), because you are the only part of SELF, Inc. that you really have to worry about.

When you get married, however, some compromises are required, because marriage involves another person's happiness equation. Those necessary compromises will limit some of your flexibility as CEO of SELF, *but* they should not eliminate your flexibility.

Building a relationship with another adult, and building a future with someone you love, is a lot different from building a relationship with a new little "bundle of joy" who can't talk, can't feed himself, and can't go to the bathroom by himself!

A child is the ultimate blessing and the ultimate challenge to both a CEO of SELF and to the marriage equation. There will not just be *some* compromises.

There will be a *lot* of compromises. The natural tendency as a new parent is to focus totally on your children's needs since they cannot meet them for themselves. However, many parents miss the transition from "needs" to "desires," (or "must-haves" versus "like-to-haves"). They become slaves to their children's desires and not just their needs. When this happens, each parent and the marriage equation come under attack.

> **A child is the ultimate blessing and the ultimate challenge to both a CEO of SELF and to the marriage equation.**

If the attack persists, both parents become SIC of SELF, and the kids become brats. We all love our kids to death. It's totally natural. We have plenty to do to take care of them until they are gradually old enough to take care of themselves. The things we have to do to take care of them are in addition to our other responsibilities—working to provide for the family, making the home comfortable, balancing the marriage equation, and then having energy and time to focus on what makes the Mom-CEO and the Dad-CEO happy. As each "bundle of joy" comes into our lives, more and more demands are placed on our time, and more and more considerations affect our dreams.

Just as kids gradually learn how to take care of themselves, they should gradually learn that there are rules, gradually learn responsibility, and understand that Mom and Dad have more voting rights than they do on the boards of MOM, Inc., DAD, Inc., and the collective HOUSEHOLD, Inc. Those are not easy lessons to teach, but they are critical to happiness for the parents and the children. Kids have to be taught certain rules and responsibilities. Don't start when the kids are sixteen and in jail.

I will never forget the time I was in Chicago O'Hare Airport waiting to board a flight, when I and everybody else in the waiting area overheard a kid, who looked to be about six years old, tell his mother, "I want my candy now, or I will start screaming!" In a panic, the mother rushed to find some candy in her purse, and then gave it to the little brat. I thought to myself, "That kid is going to grow up to be a convict."

> **Kids, in fact, will respect and respond to rules and responsibility if they learn them gradually and consistently.**

Kids, in fact, will respect and respond to rules and responsibility if they learn them gradually and consistently. I am speaking from my experience of co-raising two now responsible adults, and observing the behavior of our first grandchild, Celena—especially when she is visiting Grand-Mommy and Pa-Pa.

Celena is two years and four months old as this paragraph is being written. When she is visiting us and we are having a meal, she sits in her high chair eating her food. She's at the age when she wants to feed herself, she's starting to talk more clearly, and she's able to announce when she needs to go "potty."

A rule that we insist on, which we did with our kids when they were growing up, is that she wait until everybody else is finished eating before getting down to run around and play. Even if she does not want to eat all of her food, she must wait.

Celena has learned to respect this rule. When she has finished, she will sit, though not perfectly still, and ask me every minute or so, "Pa-Pa all done?" If I say no, she continues to wait. If Gloria looks as if she has finished eating first, Celena will ask, "Grand-Mommy all done?" Gloria might answer, "Yes, but Pa-Pa is not finished." As soon as I put my fork down or even pause, Celena will ask me again. When I finally say, "Yes, Pa-Pa all done," she smiles and starts to take off the high chair safety belt. She can be CEO of playing again!

As it was for most couples, having children was one of our dreams when Gloria and I got married, and we were blessed with Melanie and Vincent. Another one of our dreams was for them to have happy and normal childhoods, get a good education, learn to make responsible decisions in their lives, and to create and achieve their own hopes and dreams.

Gloria and I are very proud of how our kids have turned out. Both are living their own journeys. Both have retained us on their boards of directors for occasional advice, something for which we're quite thankful. And both grew out of the teenage syndrome of "parents must be the dumbest people on earth." We loved them dearly as children, and will always treasure the memories of their youth, but we are enjoying them even more as adults.

We all have a vested interest in our children, because we love them and want them to grow up to be happy and responsible adults. Our children have a vested interest in getting us to the point where we comfortably accept their "gone and on our own" approach to life. When our children learn rules and responsibility, they learn to *hope for* some things that are not just given to them, and to dream. When they learn to dream, they learn how to be happy. When they learn *how* to be happy, they become CEOs of SELF.

Championship CEO

As CEO of SELF, you are the "Michael, Martina, Wayne, Hank, Joe, Florence, and Tiger" of your dreams. Every significant achievement in the world has been made by people who believe passionately in their dream, who believe passionately in themselves. In business, these great achievers build great companies, get rich, and are called CEOs. In professional sports, they are called stars and champions.

Michael Jordan has broken so many records in professional basketball that they are doing recounts. Martina Navaratilova broke most of Billie Jean King's records in women's professional tennis and Wayne Gretzky set the record for the most number of goals scored in a professional hockey career.

When Babe Ruth retired from professional baseball with 714 career home runs, many people thought that his record would never be broken. On April 18, 1974, Hank Aaron hit career home run #715, and he ended his career with 755.

Joe Montana set a new record for the number of Super Bowl wins in professional football. And in 10.49

seconds, Florence Griffith-Joyner ("Flo-Jo") broke Evelyn Ashford's record for the 100-meter dash.

Tiger Woods has raised the level of play in professional golf so dramatically that people who can't even spell golf will watch him in person or on television when he is competing. He became a sports phenomenon as the youngest professional golfer to win a fourth major championship (the 2000 British Open). He is the youngest golfer to win all four major PGA championships. And he is the youngest golfer to hold three of the four major titles at the same time. In each case, the previous record was held by another golf phenomenon, Jack Nicklaus.

On Sunday April 8, 2001, Tiger Woods accomplished something else no other professional golfer has ever achieved. He won his *fourth* major title in a row— there are only four—when he won the 2001 Masters Tournament for the second time. His dream was to win them all, but he exceeded even his own expectations when he did it successively. There is no doubt that he is the greatest golfer on the planet, and that he has raised the bar forever.

But there is another lesson about being a champion, and it became evident during that same spectacular 2001 Masters Tournament. Phil Michelson, who finished third to Tiger, observed immediately after the competition that he had made two double bogeys and second-place finisher David Duval had recorded just one double bogey. But Tiger had made none. In other words, Tiger Woods played great *and* made fewer mistakes.

All of these athletes are champion CEOs of SELF. They had to have had dreams of playing at that level, in order to be self-motivated enough (*D-factor*) to endure training and competitive demands and pressures throughout their lives. When split second decisions could sometimes determine winning or losing, they had to be willing to take the risk of taking that last shot, or making that tournament-winning putt *(E-factor)*. They had to focus (*F-factor*) on being the *best*.

Champions don't become champions overnight. Every competitor is a barrier (*R-factor*) between champions and their dream of being the best, and in the heat of competition they must always be working on the right problems to obtain the right result (*O-factor*), which is to win. Champions inspire themselves to victory (*I-factor*), and anxious spectators into momentary euphoria. And, when champions come along and break records or move their sport to a higher level of competition, they have played great *and* made fewer mistakes . . . consistently.

> **You are the CEO of SELF, and you're in charge of your dreams. Your only competition is time, and the biggest mistake you can make is to not have a dream that's yours.**

You are the CEO of SELF, and you're in charge of your dreams. Your only competition is time, and the biggest mistake you can make is to not have a dream that's yours. When you have a dream with goals, you can best maximize your time by being the champion of your dreams. Champions do not live in their "rearview mirror," or give up when life deals them some unexpected challenges or setbacks. Champions *believe in themselves.*

At a leadership day program at the University of Nebraska at Omaha, I spoke recently to a group of high school students. My speech was about the power of dreams and goals, and how dreams come from your heart, and goals come from your head. After I spoke, one young man came up to me and said that he realized that he did have a dream, but he had not been doing all he needed to do to reach his dream. He then asked, "Is it too late?"

I responded, "Son, it's *never* too late."

Look in the mirror and see if you see a championship CEO of SELF. If you do not, it's *never* too late.

6

CEOs Anonymous

No Man Is An Island

No man is an island,
No man stands alone.
Each man's joy is joy to me,
Each man's grief is my own.
We need one another,
So I will defend,
Each man as my brother,
Each man as my friend.
— Joan Whitney and Alex Kramer

CEOs Anonymous

As a mom, wife, dad, husband, teenager, single parent, divorced parent, retiree, or any combination of these roles you might have all at once, you just might be a better CEO than many people who go to work outside their homes every day. *Why?* The extra and heavy leadership demands placed on you by virtue of those roles. All are separately challenging. The more combinations you handle simultaneously, the more challenging it is to balance the priorities in your life and to be happy.

Success at balancing the priorities and being happy starts with proclaiming that you are CEO of SELF. Members of Alcoholics Anonymous have to proclaim publicly at each meeting that they are alcoholics, which is their first step to recovery. Your first step to greater happiness is to proclaim that you are CEO of SELF! Now say it out loud!

Wife and Mom

The first big decision you made as CEO of SELF was to get married. The second big decision was to have children. After the rice was thrown and the kids started coming, you woke up one day and realized that you were in the middle of some life-changing responsibilities and commitments as a wife and mom. All combinations of roles such as wife, mom, working wife, working mom, working wife and mom are difficult at times, because each one forces some choices and tradeoffs. No matter how hard you try, there are still only twenty-four hours in a day.

Mom is the heart of the family unit. Her job is just as hard as Dad's job of bringing home the paycheck, because she is usually the first point of contact for emotional issues affecting family members on a day-to-day basis. As the kids grow up, having to deal with things like peer pressure, and finding their own identity in life, each day is an adventure for Mom. Dad's daily issues on the job can *usually* be dealt with objectively and systematically. The stay-at-home mom, on the other hand, is almost always the first to have to deal with unexpected issues affecting family members.

> **Mom is the heart of the family unit because she is usually the first point of contact for emotional issues affecting family members on a day-to-day basis.**

To handle this, Mom must be, and definitely is, a leader. First, she must be self-*motivated (D-factor)* to say "Yes" when "Mr. Right" comes along and asks her to marry him.

Advancements in medical science have taken most of the risk out of *having* a child, but there is more risk (*E-factor*) in *raising* that child to be a healthy and productive adult.

And, if Mom does not instinctively have a lot of focus (*F-factor*), it would be impossible for her to balance all of the demands on her time, attention, and affection, and still not go crazy when Dad asks where his socks are, and they are right there in front of his eyes.

Mom not only removes barriers (*R-factor*) for herself, but she is constantly removing barriers for her children, and sometimes for her husband, especially when he comes home from one of those unavoidable "bad days" at his job.

Mom also has a lot of results to obtain (*O-factor*) every day. Meal planning, food preparation, home finances, clean clothing and giving attention to each member of the family—none of these chores ever takes a vacation.

And if she gets totally disgusted with the kids, she can't just send them back to where they came from, or send out her résumé on the Internet as "Experienced Wife and Mom Looking for New Family."

Worse yet, "Mr. Right" might just turn out to be "Mr. Not-So-Right," which presents barriers beyond the scope of this book.

Still, I must remind Wife and Mom not to neglect SELF, Inc. Remember, you're well within your rights to hope for a long and happy life with "Mr. Right," but none of us knows the future. One day the kids will be grown and gone. What will you do with all that time, and where will you direct all that energy and attention?

My answer? *Your* dreams.

Wife and Mom's greatest leadership trait is her inspiration (*I-factor*) to do the things she does, and the inspiration she gives to her family. That inspiration is fueled by love, which is one of the greatest gifts God gives to man.

Being happily married and raising good kids are achievable dreams, but they undoubtedly require great women who are true CEOs of SELF. In our world, you may be anonymous CEOs to some. But, in fact, the world can't do without you.

We love you, Mom!

"Mr. Mom"

The stay-at-home dad epitomizes the concept of CEO of SELF, because of the non-traditional nature of Dad as the chief homemaker and caretaker, and Mom as the chief breadwinner.

Self-motivation (*D-factor*) and inspiration (*I-factor*) are dominant leadership characteristics required for such a role reversal, since Mr. Mom has to contend with all the challenges and demands of "Wife and Mom," plus have the inner strength to contend with the potential threat to his male ego.

Such a role reversal is sometimes made by choice, and sometimes out of necessity. With more and more women obtaining as much education as men, and often more, women are well-positioned to seize the workplace's new opportunities for themselves—opportunities that might outpace those available to their husbands. As the opportunities get bigger, pressures mount, squeezing out family quality time, and limiting time to provide guidance to the kids.

Escalating as well is pressure on women to go where the biggest opportunities are. This can often mean relocating the family to a different city, where Dad will have the responsibility of getting the kids into new schools, finding new doctors, dentists, grocery stores, and dry cleaners, and handling the myriad of other changes relocations require.

Putting aside the male ego once again, the choice to be a Mr. Mom is made based on the strength of the husband and wife relationship, *and* the life partner relationship. The husband and wife relationship is about intimacy and love. The life partner relationship is about lifestyle. The stronger the husband and wife relationship, the easier it is to make the most practical choices about who should be the primary breadwinner, and who should be the family's guiding light and stay-at-home presence—Mom or Mr. Mom.

> **The stronger the husband and wife relationship, the easier it is to make the most practical choices about who should be the primary breadwinner.**

We applaud women who can ascend to the highest ranks of business and government, because of the added challenges of succeeding in a traditionally male-dominated environment. We also applaud men who choose to be Mr. Mom. They put their commitments to their wives and to their children above any threats to their ego. In both instances, we give our sons and daughters permission to dream beyond traditional family boundaries.

Teenager

Most of us have lived through the teenage years, and you can too. The choice is what you want these years to be—a bumpy ride or smooth sailing.

As CEO of SELF, you can make your teen years go much smoother, or you can become SIC (Second-in-Command) of SELF, and bump along, hoping the wheels don't come off before you even get the car.

From the day you are born, you have the potential to be CEO of SELF. But, as you progressively learned to do more and more things for yourself, you continued to need help to survive.

Until you are mature enough to make all of your choices for yourself, and *wise enough even then to ask for advice*, obtaining guidance from those more experienced and wiser than you is a good thing to do. If you are a typical teenager, this group probably does not include *all* of your friends.

Consider carefully the advice of a sage Arabian Proverb:

> He who knows not, and knows not that he knows not,
> He is a fool, shun him.
> He who knows not, and knows that he knows not,
> He is simple, teach him.
> He who knows, and knows not that he knows,
> He is asleep, awaken him.
> He who knows, and knows he knows,
> He is wise, follow him.

Your parents or guardians are not trying to make you perfect. They are trying to help you minimize your mistakes, and maximize your future happiness. They know that, if you are not properly prepared, the world can be a cruel jungle—a place where even survival is not assured.

And though there are many things you have to deal with as a teenager, three critical rules can make your teenage years a lot smoother, and a much better preparation for a successful and happy adulthood.

As a teenager, your first rule of survival is to *have a dream*. You do not have to know how or when you're going to get there, but continually answer this question, "What is my dream?"

> **As a teenager, your first rule of survival is to *have a dream*.**

Part B of this rule is not to let friends talk you out of your dream or into something that jeopardizes it. When all is said and done, it's your life and it's your dream.

As you get older and smarter, you will discover more and more about how to make your dream come true. Along the way, you may also discover a new dream or a bigger dream. CEOs have vision, which is a dream. They need resources to reach their dream, one of which is education. The more you learn, the more excited you will be about doing the things you *have* to do, in order to achieve the things you *want* to do. Have a dream!

The second rule of teenage survival is to *accept your life* for what it is, and for what it can become. *It's not where you start in life. It's what you do with the start you have.*

You did not choose your life, but you can choose what you do with your life. You did not choose your parents or guardian, but they chose to love you. Loving you doesn't mean serving all your material wants. It means giving you emotional, psychological, and intellectual guidance. We all need love. It's human nature. Let them love you, and love them back by making the most of what you do with your life.

The third teenage survival rule is to *start now*. Every day gives you a chance to keep your life going in the right direction, or a chance to get it going in the right direction. It's okay if you're not sure what that direction is, because one of the advantages of being a teenager is that you will have many opportunities to discover new directions. No one knows how many opportunities they will be given, so just start somewhere, and start now.

> **Every day gives you a chance to keep your life going in the right direction, or a chance to get it going in the right direction.**

When I was a teenager, I felt like most teenagers feel. I was invincible and would live forever. Wrong. You aren't invincible and you won't live forever, so start using the principles for taking charge of your life discussed in chapter 8. They are just as applicable to you as a teenager. The principles are called C.E.O. *and* S.E.L.F. and here they are in abbreviated form:

C   *Communicate.* Talk to your parents and other people who are smarter than you.

E   *Evaluate.* Don't be afraid to ask questions. That's how you learn. Think for yourself.

O   *Opportunities* are everywhere if you just look for them and pursue them.

S   *Strategy*. You need one. It starts with a dream and
     education, then searching for how you get there.
E   Execution. Work at it. Success will not fall from the
     sky. You have to make it happen.
L   *Learning*. It is a continuous process throughout
     your life. It smoothes out the bumps in the road.
F   *Fun*. Yes you can have fun. Winning in life is fun.
     Losing sucks. Don't be a loser.

Life can be like riding in a new car on a smooth road
with a full tank of gas.

Or it can be like riding in an old car on a bumpy
road about to run out of gas.

The choice is yours. You are CEO of SELF.

Retiree

I was flying back from a board meeting with the CEO of
a multi-billion dollar company, who had retired from
another multi-billion dollar company a few years earlier. He had been very successful, and was very well
respected nationally as a businessman. He had plenty
of money and good health, and was in his mid-sixties at
the time.

I asked him why he had taken the new job with the
new company. When he retired, why hadn't he just
"gone fishing"? "Work," he said, "*is* my fishing."

Another friend of mine worked thirty-five years for
a railroad company as a skilled craftsman. He retired
from the company at age fifty-five, because the work
environment had deteriorated to the point where he
simply hated going to work.

He retired with enough money to live comfortably,
though not lavishly. To supplement his retirement income, he now cuts down and removes trees with a
friend of his. He works almost every day. Yet, he also

spends more time with his family, takes more mini-vacations, and has absolutely no job stress. He's created a life that he truly loves.

Whether it's making big things happen in multi-billion dollar companies or cutting down trees when you "retire," achieving happiness still requires *something to do, someone to love, and something to hope for.*

Both of my friends *do* what they want to do, have *loved* ones, and *hope* that they can continue to do what they want to do for the rest of their lives.

They demonstrate something we often forget: CEOs of SELF may retire from a job, but they never retire from life.

7

The Million Dollar Question

Success

To laugh often and much,
To win the respect of intelligent people
And the affection of children,
To earn the appreciation of honest critics
And endure the betrayal of false friends,
To appreciate beauty, to find the best in others,
To leave the world a bit better,
Whether by a healthy child or a garden patch . . .
To know that even one life has breathed easier
Because you have lived
This is to have succeeded!
—Ralph Waldo Emerson

The Million Dollar Question

Dream Search

Are you happy? That's the million-dollar question. If your answer is an unqualified *yes!*, then congratulations! You are doing the things you want to do, you have plenty of love in your life, and you have something to hope for.

If your answer to the question is a *qualified* yes, you have another question to answer. Do you want to be happier and "raise the bar?" If so, you have to go through the same process as those who answer the million-dollar question with a definitive "no." The process starts with a dream search, and as the CEO of SELF, you have to lead the search.

The most obvious place to start the search is in your heart. Throughout this book and my life, a central theme has been, *"Hope is the key to happiness, and happiness is the key to success."* What do you hope for in your heart? It may be something you used to dream about as a child or teenager, but circumstances caused you to put it aside.

That's very typical, because success is a journey, and the journey is not a straight line.

When I speak to students, one of the questions I always ask of them is, "What do you want to be when you grow up?" When I speak to adult audiences, I sometimes ask the same thing, but they think it's a trick question.

Students know they are still on their journey to success, and most of them have been asked this question before, so it makes them think about their answer.

Adults wonder why I'm asking such a dumb question. When they realize that they still have dreams in their hearts that go all the way back to when they were a child or student, they recognize that it is not such a dumb question after all.

You may have already realized some of your dreams, and others you may have just forgotten. It may not have even been a dream, but something you just always loved to do. That's a good place to start your dream search.

> **You may have already realized some of your dreams, and others you may have just forgotten. It may not have even been a dream, but something you just always loved to do. That's a good place to start your dream search.**

When I ran that first Burger King restaurant, I had to fire an assistant manager for consistently poor performance. He should have been "redirected" much earlier, but the previous management did not want to make the tough call. When I sat down with him and gave him the bad news, the young man was shocked and became emotional. After he regained his composure, we started to talk, and I asked him what he had really enjoyed doing earlier in his life.

After about a five-second pause, he said he used to love fiddling with old broken radios and TVs, and got a lot of satisfaction out of making them work again. I then asked why he had not pursued that as a career, and he said he'd never thought about it as a career and just took one of the few jobs he was offered immediately out of college. And besides, liking the job was not a big priority when he accepted the Burger King assistant manager job. He just needed a job.

After our talk, I suggested that he contact a friend of mine who worked in Human Resources at Honeywell, Inc., a computer company. He did, and after taking some technical aptitude tests, he was quickly hired and trained to be a computer repair technician. He called me a couple of years later to thank me for firing him. He had turned his "play" into "pay," and became a happy CEO of SELF.

You may not be as lucky as this young man, and your dream search may require more searching, but seeds from your childhood or earlier experiences could provide seeds of hope in finding the dream that will make you happier. Dreams come in all sizes, shapes, and speeds, so keep an open mind as you search your heart.

Technology puts your dream search at your fingertips, and it can literally span the globe. You can conduct your dream search, for example, using cable TV, learning about things you never dreamed of. Ever since CNN succeeded at 24/7 news programming, the cable services have developed a specialty channel for nearly everything under the sun. There are 24-hour news, sports, weather, cartoons, shopping, cooking, history, science and nature, science and technology, the arts, documentaries, home improvement, automotive, aviation, animals, travel, music videos, and the latest from my cable service, digital music channels. They even have digital music channels for types of music I have never heard of, such as Tejano, Folklorica, and Boleros. I must be behind the times. My next project might be a 24-hour CEO of SELF cable network.

You can also conduct your dream search using the Internet. Chat rooms and newsgroups on the Internet even allow you to talk with people you do not know about subjects you might have in common. (Warning: If there's a chat room for unhappy people, stay away from it.)

If you do not have access to the Internet, go to a library. Most of them now provide Internet access, and they still have thousands of books on everything.

> **A dream search can start in your heart, your head, from TV or radio, from an article in a newspaper or magazine, on the Internet, on your job, in a conversation, gazing at the stars, or in a dream.**

In fact, a dream search can start in your heart, your head, from TV or radio, from an article in a newspaper or magazine, on the Internet, on your job, in a conversation, gazing at the stars, or in a dream. The key, however, is persistence. A very familiar and famous song has a passage that may say it best, "Climb every mountain, ford every stream, follow every rainbow, 'til you find your dream."

If you want an excuse for not being happier, you can find one. CEOs do not look for excuses. They look for dreams and the "happiness zone."

The Happiness Zone

Happiness is a *zone*. The objective is to get into, and stay in, the happiness zone as much as possible.

Unhappiness is also a zone, which can be created by a multitude of factors, such as the loss of a loved one, seeing a loved one who is unhappy, or just habit. My two-year old granddaughter, Celena, is a typical, happy child with a very happy personality. If she is unhappy about something other than being hungry or some other physical discomfort, it rips my heart out. And, as you would expect, "Pa-Pa" wants to fix it to make her happy.

> **Happiness is a *zone*. The objective is to get into, and stay in, the happiness zone as much as possible.**

There is also a middle zone called "not happy/not unhappy." My executive assistant, Sibby, pointed this out to me one day after trying to explain to her daughter that there are times in life when you are in the middle zone, no matter how much you try to be in the happiness zone. You're not unhappy. You're just not happy at that moment.

She's right! That's when I started to realize, even more so than before, that happiness and leadership are "joined at the hip." Just as a CEO has to constantly work at sustaining success, you have to constantly work at staying in the happiness zone. Athletes, for example, can get in a zone. They don't get in that zone in every game or tournament, but it happens. I remember watching Michael Jordan play basketball in a televised game one day. As the commentators would say, he was "on fire." He just seemed to sink every shot he made. After one particularly unbelievable shot, Michael, passing in front of the camera, just shrugged his shoulders as if to say even he was in disbelief that that last shot had gone in. Michael was *in the zone.* He knew he was in the zone. An athlete is *in the zone* when exceptional conscious ability and exceptional subconscious execution come together.

> **A CEO of SELF is in the happiness zone when dreams and goals come together, and the CEO is in the right position to succeed.**

A CEO of SELF is in the happiness zone when dreams and goals come together, and the CEO is in the right position to succeed. Staying in your *happiness zone* or getting out of the *unhappiness zone* is a leadership challenge. People in the happiness zone most of the time are there because they work at it. If they slip into the middle or unhappiness zone, they make no excuses and waste no time before they take charge and lead themselves back into the happiness zone as CEO of SELF. This is the same challenge a CEO has when a business is trying to sustain its success, or is in trouble. In either case, the CEO *removes identified barriers to self-motivation, works on the right problems, and inspires himself.*

> **The CEO *removes identified barriers to self-motivation, works on the right problems, and inspires himself.***

The Million-Dollar J.O.B.

Most people need a job to support themselves and their families, and if they are really successful, they may even have enough left over to satisfy some of their desires beyond the basics. A job also gives people something to do, which itself is a key component of happiness.

But not everyone is happy with or in love with the job they have. Some like their job. Others hate their job.

If you love your job, congratulations! You *have* a "million-dollar job," even if you don't earn a lot of money. Income alone does not make you love your job. You think of your "J.O.B." as "Just Outstanding and Better" every-day, instead of "Just Ordinary and Boring." For you, it's not a job, it's a *j-ahh-b!*

Some people who "like" their job think they'd love it if it suddenly paid them a million dollars a year. Not necessarily. People with actual million-dollar-a-year jobs have walked away from them, primarily because they, as CEOs of SELF, did not love what they were doing, and in fact were either unhappy doing it, or actually hated the job itself. Granted, they had probably saved enough money to walk away, but they did walk away in order to be happier, and, given the stress reduction, probably added years to their lives.

If you like your job, ask yourself what could make you love it, and then turn it into a *j-ahh-b!* If there is something within your control, why not do it? You are, after all, the CEO of SELF.

> **If you like your job, ask yourself what could make you love it, and then turn it into a *j-ahh-b!***

When I graduated from high school, I got a summer job as a laborer for a housing project under construction. They assigned me to a "Mr. Rogers" to help him dig out a section of the concrete floor in one of the buildings using a jackhammer. I had never used a jackhammer before, but it didn't look too difficult and, after he gave me a brief lesson, he put me on the jackhammer, and kept me on it all day. When I got home that night, I was too tired to eat and my head was ringing from the noise. I finally ate dinner and went to bed, so I could work with "Mr. Rogers" again the next day. After that experience, I came to one big conclusion in my life: I am the CEO of SELF and I will finish college even if it kills me! I hated that job.

People who hate their jobs are constantly stressed, which is not healthy. Circumstances may prevent you from just walking away, but you can look for ways to reduce some of the stress. If the problem is a boss or a colleague, then maybe a "heart to heart" talk might help you at least to coexist. If you tried that and it did not work, you should already be working on a plan to get out of there. (If the work itself is the problem, then you need the plan anyway.)

Another common circumstance is the amount of time invested in the job, which may place you too close to retirement to leave. In that case, your dream is retirement. So focus on the dream rather than the "potholes."

> **In trying to make your job less ordinary and more interesting, another option is to focus on the "cans" and not the "cannots."**

In trying to make your job less ordinary and more interesting, another option is to focus on the "cans" and not the "cannots." Some bosses think their job is to tell people what they can and cannot do, and then spend more time on the "cannots," which makes people afraid to make a mistake. But you can choose to focus on the "cans," which can positively affect your attitude, and possibly the attitude of others around you. When you choose to focus on the "cans," you are also making the choice to exceed expectations, rather than just meet them.

Return with me again to my first Burger King restaurant. When the district manager told me that I was being given the responsibility to manage the restaurant (although I thought of it as being CEO of the restaurant),

I asked him to explain his expectations of me. "Just increase the sales and the profits," he said. When I asked if could change any of the menu prices, he said I could not. I asked if I could spend some discretionary marketing dollars. He said nope. I asked if I could eliminate the Parmesan sandwich from the menu, since we only sold two a month. He again said no. Everything I asked about was a big fat "cannot."

As I took charge of the restaurant, I started to think about one thing he did not put in the "cannot" category. He did not say I could not change the attitude of everybody in the restaurant. I had remembered from "Burger Boot Camp" at Burger King University (yes, there is one) how much they emphasized telling the cashiers to smile, to get customers to smile, in order to make them feel like coming back. I noticed a lot of my cashiers were not smiling either, and so a lot of the customers were not smiling. This is when I created the BEAMER program, which taught people (mostly teenagers) how to make people smile.

Look people in the eye and smile, and they will smile back.

Unless someone is among the walking dead, it works every time.

When I took over as manager of the restaurant, its end-of-year sales projection was about $800,000. After three months of the BEAMER program, the district manager (Mr. "Cannots") revised the projection upwards to one million dollars, since the sales trend had moved up noticeably. (I still had the Parmesan sandwich on the menu.)

Work is a big part of what we do in life to live and be happy. Most primary breadwinners in a household will work about forty-five years before "retirement." You may not always be able to choose that dream job or control your circumstances, which can get you stuck in a job, but you can choose to be CEO of your attitude in every job you have.

A million-dollar attitude can change a job into a *j-ahh-b*—one that is "Just Outstanding and Better" everyday!

The Other Question

Dr. Mays reminds us that, "We make our living by what we get, but we make our life by what we give." Everyone must not only search for their dreams and happiness, but for what gives their life meaning. As pointed out earlier, Reiss's value-based happiness is a sense that our lives have meaning and fulfill some larger purpose, and that there is no limit to how meaningful our lives can be. The more we give, the more our lives have meaning.

> **Everyone must not only search for their dreams and happiness, but for what gives their life meaning.**

Some people find life's meaning by dedicating themselves to helping others meet basic needs, such as Mother Teresa, who was admired throughout the world for always putting the needs of those *most in need* over her own desires or comfort. Or, take my friend Joe Edmonson, whose trampoline accident left him a quadriplegic. He and his wife Jean started a youth outreach center in Omaha, Nebraska to give kids from economically challenged homes a sense of belonging and purpose when the home was fatherless, or motherless or both. After his accident, Joe focused on his "cans" instead of his "cannots."

Some spouses are the unsung heroes and heroines of successful people, who give a lot to life and are also able to sustain a happy and functional family. Most successful CEOs have a strong and supportive vice-chairman, who adds meaning to their success and their life.

Still others find life's meaning by creating wealth and resources that assist other people through charitable organizations they establish. Warren Buffett, for example, says he will leave his multi-billions to a foundation, which will work for the public and social good. I know Warren. And I know he believes that making money should help make people's lives better.

Yes, we all lead fast and busy lives, and life is getting faster and faster, and busier and busier. But as Emerson says in his poem,

> *To leave the world a bit better,*
> *Whether by a healthy child or a garden patch . . .*
> *To know that even one life has breathed easier*
> *Because you have lived,*
> *This is to have succeeded!*

What are you giving back?

That's the "other question."

8

Taking Charge

Believe In Yourself

Believe there's a reason to be,
believe you can make time stand still,
and know from the moment you try,
if you believe, you know you will.

Believe in yourself, right from the start,
believe in the magic, there in your heart,
believe all these things, not because I told you to.
But, believe in yourself, believe in yourself,
believe in yourself, as God believes in you.
—From the Broadway musical, "The Wiz"

Taking Charge

Your Choice

The CEO of SELF principles of happiness and success will affect the choices you make for the rest of your life. Let's summarize these principles before you take charge.

- Happiness is something to do, someone to love, and something to hope for.
- Hope is the key to happiness, which is the key to success.
- Success is a journey, not a destination.
- The road to happiness and success is not straight.
- Being in position to succeed is being on the right road.
- That road will always have speed bumps, potholes, and detours.
- CEOs remove barriers, obtain results, and inspire themselves
- You are CEO of SELF. Choose to take charge.

Life is about choices.

You choose to get married, have children, have a career, be a supportive spouse, put your children first, dedicate your life to helping others, work for the same company as long as you can, or start your own business.

These are among the many decisions you make along your journey through life.

Each decision enhances your level of happiness and success, or it makes your life more complicated. In either case, you are where you are. The question is, "Do you want to change?" If you do, it's *your* choice. It may not require changing everything. It may necessitate changing only one thing. Just as people are motivated by the desire to satisfy their unmet needs successively (Maslow's hierarchy), people become happier and more successful by making changes in their lives one at a time.

> **Each decision enhances your level of happiness and success, or it makes your life more complicated.**

The choices you make for the rest of your life will depend on a lot of factors. One big factor is time. You may think you do not have time to make a lot of changes in your life. Or you may think you have all the time in the world. Your perspective toward change, I've found, is largely generational. I call them the K, X, Y, Z, and G generations.

The G generation are the "grown folks." They range in age from fifty-six on up. Their perspective is predominantly to "survive," because many of them lived through the Great Depression of the 1930s, and they want to be prepared if times that hard come again.

The Z generation is made up of the "baby boomers," ages thirty-six to fifty-five. Their perspective is to "thrive," because they have been the primary beneficiaries of the great prosperity of the last fifty years.

The Y generation—those between the ages of twenty-six and thirty-five—are the "glide" generation. They will eventually get their feet on the ground, but they are not in any particular hurry to do so.

The X generation is the "drive" generation. Between the ages of fifteen and twenty-six years of age, they are just driving through life in somebody else's car, and believe they have all the time in the world to reach their destination.

The K generation are the kids fourteen years old and under. They are the "ride" generation because they don't care who's driving or whose car they're in. They're along for the ride and loving every minute of it.

> **Whether you are usually in the happiness, unhappiness, or middle zone, there are always choices to be made, and you must choose to take charge as CEO of SELF.**

Your generational perspective, and the perspective of your stockholders, will affect your life choices. You are either happy with your life, unhappy with your life, or in the middle zone—neither happy nor unhappy. Whether you are usually in the happiness, unhappiness, or middle zone, there are always choices to be made, and you must choose to take charge as CEO of SELF. It's always your choice.

Taking charge of SELF, Inc. involves the same process as taking charge of a business. I call the process C.E.O. *and* S.E.L.F. My experiences at Godfather's Pizza, Incorporated will illustrate the process.

C.E.O. *and* S.E.L.F. at GPI

Communications, Evaluation, and Opportunities

The Pillsbury Board of Directors approved my appointment as president of Godfather's with an effective date of April 1, 1986. My boss, Jeff Campbell, had issued an official communication to all employees, franchise owners, suppliers, distributors, and the media about one week earlier. I was now in charge.

Jeff had offered to fly to Omaha with me to introduce me to the corporate staff, but I declined his offer, because I knew he had a lot more important things to do than a trip for a "meet and greet."

Jeff also knew that I had never been shy about introducing myself when I was put in charge of something, so he had one of the vice presidents pick me up at the airport.

When I arrived at the office, I was introduced to Ron Gartlan, executive vice president of the company. Ron and I met for a while, and I asked him to call a meeting of all employees in the corporate office for that afternoon. I wanted to introduce myself to them, and let them know what to expect over the next several weeks.

That afternoon, at a meeting of about a hundred people, I walked in with Ron, who introduced me very briefly as the new president. I started to address the group and told them a little about my history with Pillsbury, my background, and what I would be doing to get familiar with them and the business. But the most important thing I told them was that I did not have all the answers to the challenges we faced. They did. My job was to ask them the right questions so, together, we could make the company successful again.

My next step in the communications process was a series of one-on-one meetings with the top twenty-five managers at the company. These ninety-minute meetings occupied most of my first few days. I started with Ron that same evening over dinner, where we talked extensively about his perspectives on company issues and personnel.

The one-on-one meetings were not just a formality. They gave me an opportunity to hear first-hand each person's opinions about the issues we faced and the direction we should take.

Secondly, conducting these meetings sent a message that their opinions were important. In each of the meetings, I started the discussion by asking the same three questions: "What's your history and background with GPI?" "What would you do if you were the new president?" "What are your goals and aspirations?" The responses were a starting point for developing some strategic initiatives to focus on, and a starting point for an evaluation of the available management talent.

I asked similar questions of the franchise owners I talked with during those first few weeks, which further validated the collective input I had received earlier. Not all of the input I received those first few weeks was exactly the same, but some clear consistency of opinions was emerging, and my job was to pull everything together into a coherent plan.

As the communications process continued, I also evaluated the restaurant operations, the physical facilities, and the financial resources we would have available to turn the business around. I was particularly attentive to what seemed like previously unexplored opportunities, especially those that might be called "low hanging fruit." One such idea was to eliminate three of our pizza crust variations to greatly simplify the day-to-day operations. Phasing out the remaining inventories of flour required no investment, and practically no time. The management team and some of the franchise owners had made this suggestion to me, and I liked it.

Many "low hanging fruit" opportunities evolved out of this process, as well as many opportunities requiring more time and capital to implement. But the biggest opportunity to emerge came from the belief by nearly all constituencies that we could achieve the dream of making the company profitable again. This was a win-win for everyone.

Strategy, Execution, Learning, and Fun

Jeff had asked me to develop a *strategic* plan within one hundred days of taking over. I was able to develop the new plan in only sixty days, because there were a lot of good ideas just "lying around"—ideas the previous president had been reluctant to decide on or implement. I did not have that problem.

In order to officially launch the *execution* of the new plan, and to provide an opportunity for all of the stakeholders in Godfather's to hear from the "new sheriff," we held an all-systems meeting sixty days after my arrival. It was an upbeat and inspiring meeting! People were enthusiastic about the company's new direction, because it reflected a consensus of opinions and suggestions shared by a large number of people in the company. After the meeting, one franchise owner told me he was glad that I was not afraid to make a decision. I thanked him, but pointed out that not everyone would like some of the decisions I would have to make in the future, as we learned more and more about what we needed to do to succeed. We did not have all the answers after sixty days, but we had some, and we had a lot more questions.

> **A strategic plan is not a perfect set of steps. It is a guide in the *learning* process.**

A strategic plan is not a perfect set of steps. It is a guide in the *learning* process. As you execute the plan, you learn more and more about what works and what does not, which allows you to continuously refine tactics to make them work better. The more of our 725 restaurants I visited, and the more of the 12,000 company-affiliated people I personally met, the more I learned about the difficult decisions I had to make. We would eventually close two hundred of our restaurants. Those decisions, I can assure you, were not popular across-the-board.

But overall, our strategy worked. We began winning again, and winning is *fun*. Pillsbury, the employees, franchise owners, suppliers, distributors, customers, and the "new sheriff"—all of us were excited about seeing our vision of success become a reality.

Taking charge of a company, a region, a restaurant, a department, or a project involves the process of:

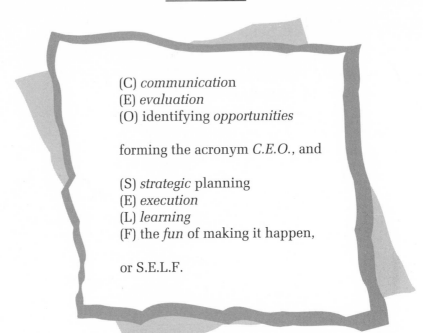

(C) *communication*
(E) *evaluation*
(O) identifying *opportunities*

forming the acronym *C.E.O.*, and

(S) *strategic* planning
(E) *execution*
(L) *learning*
(F) the *fun* of making it happen,

or S.E.L.F.

Taking charge of your success and happiness as CEO of SELF requires the same steps, but you must choose to take them.

C.E.O. *and* S.E.L.F. for SELF, Inc.

Communication, Evaluation, and Opportunities

Communication is the key to a successful relationship between a company and its employees, a CEO and his or her directors, a husband and wife, parents and children, or sisters and brothers. Good communication can ease tensions that naturally crop up because of fear, uncertainty, and change. Good communication helps to refocus all stockholders on the right priorities, rather than on change itself.

Taking charge of your happiness as CEO of SELF is not about giving a family member or boss a piece of your mind. Taking charge begins with planning to communicate, and developing a communications plan.

The communication plan for your family stockholders could include an official announcement during an initial group meeting that you want everyone in the family to be happier, and that all of you are going to work together to make that happen.

You could then begin the discussion with your "state of the family" and "state of your happiness" reports, after which you could request feedback from each family member. I strongly recommend having someone take notes, so the discussion can be summarized later, because some people remember only what they want to remember.

> **The most common mistake, however, is to assume that everyone knows everyone else's feelings, goals, and dreams.**

Some people hold family stockholder meetings on a regular basis. For them, only a communications "tune-up" on one or two topics may be required. The most common mistake, however, is to assume that everyone knows everyone else's feelings, goals, and dreams. Most of us never articulate our goals and dreams aloud, so it should come as no surprise that others don't know what they are.

Separate meetings may be required for immediate family stockholders, parental stockholders, siblings, and extended family members such as aunts and uncles, because the issues and opportunities to be discussed are usually very different for each group. The common denominator is you, which is why the CEO of SELF must take the lead to achieve happier stockholders for a happier you.

When he was living in Atlanta, my brother Thurman was able and willing to help our mother with things she could not do for herself as she got older and MS continued to limit her physically. Also helping look after Mom's needs were Uncle Ned and Aunt Retha, who had retired from work about ten years earlier, and settled in Atlanta. They had always been close to Mom and became even closer after they moved.

Since Thurman's death, Uncle Ned and Aunt Retha have done even more to help Mom. That they established a wonderful, mutually supportive relationship gave me a lot of peace of mind about Mom's care when I was living in Omaha. Indeed, I'll forever be grateful for their support of Mom.

But, after moving back to Atlanta, I did not just assume that everybody was happy. I met and talked with Uncle Ned and Aunt Retha to make sure that they did not feel imposed upon due simply to circumstances. They assured me that they were very happy with the situation. I also talked to Mom, and she was equally happy.

Although Uncle Ned and Aunt Retha are a little younger than Mom, I wanted to make it easier for them to continue to help Mom as they got older, which was also helpful to me given my demanding travel schedule. At age seventy-six, and despite MS, Mom still likes her independence, so the idea of living with Uncle Ned and Aunt Retha did not go very far with her.

But when a condominium across the hall from Mom's became available, I jumped at the opportunity to ask Uncle Ned and Aunt Retha if they wanted to move into it, since it was bigger than the apartment they had currently, and since living there would bring them much closer to Mom. They loved the idea, so I assisted them in acquiring the condo. Uncle Ned said later that even though they are *close* to Mom, being across the hall was close enough.

The one-on-one meetings with Uncle Ned and Aunt Retha, and then with Mom, are similar to the meetings I held with each of the members of the GPI management team when I took charge of Godfather's. You may want to do the same thing with your primary stockholders to show that they and their opinions are important to you, to make certain that no one feels taken for granted, and to make sure you are working on the right problems and opportunities.

> **Good communication does not start with, "When I get around to it." It starts with, "Let's talk."**

These one-on-one meetings do not have to be "office visits." You can take advantage of any opportunity for private discussion, such as a car ride or a sports activity. They can include going for a walk together, standing around the grill and chatting while the ribs are cooking, or having a one-on-one meal together.

Good communication does not start with, "When I get around to it." It starts with, "Let's talk," a desire to communicate, and a communications plan.

What is the biggest issue or opportunity you need to discuss with your spouse, your children, your parents, your grandparents, your siblings, or your aunts or uncles? Most issues do not just go away, and most opportunities have only a short "window" to pursue. The CEO starts the communication process, which, at his insistence, becomes ongoing in nature.

If you encounter serious communication barriers that you can't overcome on your own, you may want to seek professional help. The objective is to make everyone happier, with a better understanding of everyone's respective situation, goals, and dreams, which includes those of the CEO—you.

> **The objective is to make everyone happier, with a better understanding of everyone's respective situation, goals, and dreams, which includes those of the CEO—you.**

The *evaluation* process should be also ongoing in nature, because it will allow you to continuously resolve issues (remove barriers) and identify new *opportunities.* You have to continuously consider changes in the family, changes in health, changes in financial conditions, changes at work, and external changes which can affect your goals, dreams, success, and happiness. Evaluation of these and other changes requires deliberate attention, because it is especially easy for family members to be so caught up in their individual activities that they stay connected only "on the fly."

When Melanie and Vincent were growing up, we made it a practice to have most evening meals together.

During dinner, we allowed no TV, no radio, no CD players, and no video games—in fact, nothing that distracted from quality family conversation. If it was quiet, that was okay, but it usually did not stay quiet for very long in the Cain family. These regular family chats proved very effective in staying connected to changes in each other's lives and each other's feelings.

Communication, evaluation, and *opportunities* with your place of employment shareholders may also require you to take charge as CEO of SELF. Most businesses provide their people with periodic performance evaluations, which are intended to be two-way communications and evaluations. Some companies and bosses are better at this discipline than others. If your job is a *j-aah-b* as discussed in chapter 7, then there's no problem. If your job is just a job, then you will have to pursue some of the suggestions also discussed in chapter 7.

> **A good balance between the interests of employer and family shareholders is critical to achieving a balance between success *and* happiness for the CEO of SELF.**

The employer-shareholder component of your success and happiness should be shared with your family shareholders as much as practical, because a good balance between the interests of employer and family shareholders is critical to achieving a balance between success *and* happiness for the CEO of SELF.

Strategy, Execution, Learning, and Fun

The communication, evaluation, and opportunities phases will allow you to gather a great many opinions, suggestions, and ideas. You should then combine this with your own independent research and opinions to develop a *strategy*, and the specific tactics for the *execution* phase.

> **A strategy consists of broad directional initiatives toward your dream, whereas tactics are specific tasks for each strategic initiative.**

A strategy consists of broad directional initiatives toward your dream, whereas tactics are specific tasks for each strategic initiative. For example, when my dream was to become president of some existing corporate entity, my strategy was to:

- Stay with Pillsbury
- Transfer to the restaurant division
- Work my way back up to VP, and all the while
- Perform outstandingly

Because the president of Pillsbury had told me that there was a shortage of good management talent in the restaurant division due to its anticipated growth, I had concluded that outstanding performance might give me a shot at the presidency of one of the restaurant companies. There was no guarantee, but at least *I would be in position to reach my dream*. The division's anticipated growth would create many new opportunities, but I had to be in position to take advantage of them.

Not all of the tactics necessary for each strategic initiative will be immediately obvious to you. Some things you learn as you go, as you explore opportunities, as conditions change, and as you pursue each strategic step.

The tactics for each step of the previous examples were the following, with those in *italics* discovered along the way.

- ▶ Stay with Pillsbury
  Don't get fired
  Don't quit
- ▶ Transfer to the Restaurant Division
  Identify possible opportunity
  Look into Burger King "Fast Track" Program
  Evaluate financial impact
  Evaluate impact on family
  Evaluate potential timing
  Make a decision
- ▶ Work my way back up to VP
  Don't look back
  Work a little harder and longer
  Survive resentment, sabotage, and conspiracy
  Complete operations training
  Wait for Region VP assignment
- ▶ Perform outstandingly
  Take charge of Philadelphia Region
  Identify critical problems
  Identify "low hanging fruit" opportunities
  Develop plan and execute consistently
  Survive resentment, sabotage, and conspiracy

When I needed to identify a possible opportunity, I was able to meet with the president of the Bennigan's Restaurant Division, and the president of Burger King, Inc. The meeting with Bennigan's president, Hal Smith, was informative and cordial, but there was no immediately obvious way to bring me into the business without a lot of concessions on my part. I expected to make some concessions, but not a 60 percent pay cut, a relocation of my family, and working like a dog to prove myself all over again. Many years later, Hal told me that he really did not know at the time what to do with a guy who was willing to give up a VP job at Pillsbury, and to go to work in a restaurant.

My meeting with Lou Neeb, president of Burger King, uncovered BK's fast track program. The company was growing so fast that the organization was unable to generate RVP candidates with the necessary operational and leadership experience. The fast track program was designed to provide accelerated operations experience to people with seasoned leadership experience.

The program was relatively new, and by the time I started it, Lou had left Burger King. The new Burger King president also supported the program, because he had been one of the few people to go through it successfully. His name was Jeff Campbell.

The meeting with my family stockholders to consider the decision of going to Burger King was with my wife and vice chairman of the board, Gloria. Melanie and Vincent were not voting members yet, since, at the time, they were nine and three years old, respectively. Gloria and I had had previous discussions about my ambition to become president of something, so this discussion was more about what changes would be required.

We would not have to relocate until after my training, which I would be doing in Minneapolis, where we were then living. My work schedule would be drastically different, including some nights and weekends, and I would have to take a 20 percent cut in pay . . . though only temporarily.

Gloria never doubted that I would succeed in the program, and I never doubted myself, either. We both also knew that in the unlikely event that this did not work out, and I needed a job to feed the family, there was a ditch out there somewhere that needed digging.

Joining Burger King solidified the *execution* phase of my strategy, because these changes were real. It was a real resignation from Pillsbury, a real change in work, real risks, and a real 20 percent pay cut of real money. But, it was also a real opportunity to be in position to achieve my dream.

Our lifestyle did not change much. We were still living our lives pretty much the same as before. We were still *learning* a lot, still having *fun* raising two children, still taking real vacations, and still looking to the future optimistically. The biggest adjustment was the uncertainty in my schedule from week to week, since I was a trainee, and then later an assistant manager. But when I became manager of the restaurant, I was *in charge* of the schedule.

Executing my strategy at Burger King and then later becoming president of Godfather's put me in position to exceed even my own expectations. Pursuing my dreams and the things I have wanted for my family has always been fun for me. Maybe I'm the exception, but I have never been afraid to be in charge of a project, a group, a restaurant, a region, a company, an association, or, most importantly, to be in charge as CEO of SELF.

One of the other reasons I worked so hard and made my numerous career changes was to be able to enjoy with my family some of the things Dad did not get a chance to enjoy. When his health was getting worse and he was hospitalized, he told me to enjoy my success along the way, not to save it up for a day I might never see.

When our daughter Melanie graduated from college, we took a family vacation in Maui, Hawaii, and I told Vincent we would do the same when he graduated from college. It was *fun* to see him walk down the aisle with the other graduates recently, and it was fun to be back in Maui. In fact, it was even more fun because of the addition of our son-in-law Cesare and our first grandchild, Celena Patrice.

Your Move

Your life may seem to be complicated by increasing demands on your time and conflicting priorities, and there are still only twenty-four hours in each day. Some of these conflicting priorities are:

- Spend quality time with your family, but succeed at work.
- Be a good mom and wife, but make mom happy too.
- Give your kids a little better start in life than you had, but don't spoil them.
- Work hard, but take some time off.
- Spend for today, but save for tomorrow.
- Eat healthy, but don't eat too much.
- Lose some weight, but don't be too skinny.
- Get more exercise, but don't hurt yourself.
- Speed up, but slow down.

Life is about choices *and* balance, success *and* happiness.

The only person who can see the world and your dreams through your eyes is you, CEO of SELF. The Planning Guide at the end of this chapter can help you get started.

As you make your move, always remember these words:

"Believe there's a reason to be,
believe you can make time stand still,
and know from the moment you try,
if you believe, you know you will.

Believe in yourself, right from the start,
believe in the magic, there in your heart,
believe all these things, not because I told you
  to.
But, believe in yourself, believe in yourself,
believe in yourself, as God believes in you."

CEO of SELF Strategic Planning Guide

Operating Instructions

At the end of this exercise, you will have identified what it's going to take to be a better CEO of SELF. It starts with a plan or even an idea of where you are, where you are going, and how you plan to get there.

The first time through, you may not have all the answers to all the questions—in fact, you probably won't. But continue the process until you have established your direction in your heart and in your mind. At that point, this guide becomes your report card, and use it to grade your progress.

You may not want to immediately share these answers with all of your stockholders and advisors, because some of your honest answers may touch on highly sensitive subjects. Those sensitive areas can be better addressed at a later time.

After you have answered all of the questions to the best of your ability, then take the advice of my grandfather, "sleep on it" for a couple of days. You will then be ready to "take charge."

ASK THE RIGHT QUESTIONS TO *OBTAIN* THE RIGHT RESULTS

1. What three things in your life make you really happy?

_____

_____

_____

2. What three things would you most like to change?

_____

_____

_____

3. What is YOUR dream? (*Say it out loud.*)

4. What is your "decade goal?" (*Say it out loud.*)

5. Are you "in position" to reach your dream? If yes, then skip to #9. If no, then go to #6.

REMOVE BARRIERS

6. What three things will get you in position to achieve your goals and reach your dream?

_____

_____

_____

7. What are the "pluses" and "minuses" of each option? (Write down the pros and cons on separate sheets.)

8. Which option are you most and least comfortable with?

9. What three specific goals must you accomplish to move you toward your dream?

_____

_____

_____

10. What will be your plan for communicating your strategy?

INSPIRE THYSELF

11. What is your source of daily inspiration? (*Do it every day.*)

12. Do you really, truly believe in yourself?

9

Questions You Had to Ask

Ask In Faith

"If any of you lack wisdom, let him ask of God,
That giveth to all men liberally, and unbraideth not;
And it shall be given him.
But let him ask in faith, nothing wavering."
— James 1:5–6

Questions You Had to Ask

1. At what early age should people begin forming, articulating, and pursuing their dreams and goals?

There is no magic age. As children, we learn to dream. We also learn that sometimes we have to do certain things to get what we want. As children, for example, we learn to eat our vegetables in order to get dessert, which is a very short-term goal. As we get older, our goals become larger and farther out in time, and soon we have both goals and dreams. One year, I dreamed of getting a new bicycle for Christmas. I knew—or thought I knew—that unless I was "good" all year, Santa Claus would not bring me that bike. When I learned the real deal about Santa, and that I could not just wish for stuff, I started to develop grown-up dreams.

2. You say that you had a decade goal of achieving a $20,000 a year salary by age thirty. What were some of your earlier goals and did you achieve them?

The decade goals started after college. Prior to that, my goals were determined more by where I was in school. For example, I wanted to be elected student body president in the seventh grade, but I lost to the most popular athlete.

In high school, I wanted to excel in band, so I started working my way up from last trombone to first trombone. I actually had started playing the trombone in eighth grade, and learned to outplay all the other trombone players by the start of tenth. It just took a lot of practice.

I also wanted to be student body president in high school. That time, I ran and won, defeating the school's most popular athlete.

In college, my dream was simply to graduate. No one in our family had ever gone that far in school, and I figured I needed more education to make more money.

In college, I also wanted to make the glee club's traveling group, which went on tour each year to different parts of the country. More than one hundred students took part in the glee club, but only forty were selected for the tour based on individual auditions. I was selected all four years. In my senior year, I was also elected glee club president, and asked to sing in the prestigious Morehouse College Quartet.

3. Is there anything wrong with setting goals more frequently than every decade—like every five years?
There's nothing at all wrong with setting goals more frequently than every decade. It just depends on how big you want to dream. Big dreams take longer. They might require twenty years instead of ten. In either case, some short-term goals should be part of your bigger overall goal. How far apart you spread your goals depends on you, the person, and your dream. Ten year goals work for me.

4. You didn't seem to have dreams/goals about getting married and having children. What's the distinction between personal and professional goals?

I certainly did have dreams of getting married and having children, and those dreams came true. The distinction between personal and professional goals is that personal goals are influenced more by internal factors, whereas professional goals are heavily affected by external factors. Yet, they complement each other. If I had not had my family to share my success with, I probably would not have been as successful as I have been, and certainly not as happy.

5. Have you ever had to compromise your beliefs in order to succeed?

The answer is, "Absolutely not." I have never compromised my faith, my morals, or my beliefs in order to succeed. Young people have the misperception that it's necessary to be ruthless in order to get ahead in the corporate business world. I emphasize to them that they always have a choice—the choice to walk away, and the choice to change jobs—so they don't have to compromise their integrity.

6. Is it inappropriate to declare, for example, that you want to be a multi-millionaire by age thirty, or forty, or fifty? If it is, does it matter?

No, I don't think it's inappropriate to make such a declaration, because money can be a liberating factor. It can allow people to pursue non-material things that they believe in. For example, money was a means for my Dad to liberate himself from poverty and to liberate his kids from a potential lack of educational opportunity. By the same token, I greatly admire Steve Forbes.

He was willing to spend a lot of his own money to run for president because he wanted to help fix some of our nation's biggest problems.

7. Did you actually have a dream of being a book writer or a keynote speaker, or both?
No, I could never have dreamed of being either one. When I started high school, my grammar was very poor, which made me very self-conscious when I spoke extemporaneously in front of people. And in college, I did not pass my composition course the first time I took it, so I was forced to take it again.

8. How did you go from a high school student with poor speaking skills to a career as a highly sought after professional keynote speaker and the author of three books?
Focus. Focus. Focus.
Hard work. Hard work. Hard work.
Determination. Determination. Determination.
At different stages of my life, I was driven by a desire to succeed. Along the way, I discovered that keynote speaking and writing were critical to my success.

9. Can you have a dream and still not be CEO of SELF?
Yes. If you have a dream and do nothing about it, then you are not being CEO of SELF.

10. Can you be a CEO of SELF and not have a dream?
No. CEOs have a direction and focus, which are defined by their goals and dreams.

11.What happens to CEOs of SELF if they set a dream, but fail to achieve it? Must they then perpetually supply a new deadline for it? Are the CEOs of SELF destroyed by regularly failing to achieve their dream?

Dreams can be far-reaching, but they must also be realistic. If you are not properly positioned to reach your dream, you're being unrealistic. Achieving your dream is hard work, which is why some people just dream and never try. There is no harm in changing the time horizon for reaching your dream, but there is harm in having no dream. Changing your timetable should not destroy you as a person, because the power of the dream should be much stronger than how long it takes to achieve it.

12. Is there danger if people achieve their dreams in a ruthless and unethical manner?

Compassion for other people (someone to love) is a big part of happiness. If we achieve our dreams in a ruthless manner—a manner that hurts people—we may not be happy when and if we get there. I have only run into a few people who were openly unethical or deceitful in their pursuits. Their lack of character and principles eventually caught up with them.

13. Isn't there a big danger when people promise themselves they'll be happy if they achieve their dream, but still aren't happy when they do?

There is never a danger in achieving your dream. Some people are just unable to be happy. If that's the case, they have bigger problems than I'm qualified to address.

14. Aren't you, unusual, Herman—that is, specially gifted, so that this program only works for you?

We are all blessed with some raw talents. The *ideas* in this book can work for anyone, if they choose to adapt them to their talents and their life.

15. You place a lot of emphasis on God. If I'm an atheist or an agnostic, or simply less devout than you, will your advice still work for me?

More people minimize their potential by not believing in themselves than by not believing in God. Things are just harder without God.

16. What do you do if you declare a dream and, no matter how persuasive you are, your spouse completely disagrees with it?

Sometimes you have to agree to disagree. Love does not mean total agreement all of the time, but it does mean respecting each other's differences. When disagreeing on a dream, the two spouses must make a choice based on how each analyzes the pros and cons. In the end, it still has to be your decision.

17. Have you been unhappy even once in your life?

Yes, a few times that I can remember, but I ain't tellin'.

18. Did your spouse work, and how did that affect your dreams—setting and achieving them?

Before our children were born, Gloria worked briefly as a teacher and a librarian. When the kids were born, she chose not to work, and instead to be a supportive wife, a mom, and a homemaker. Her choices were a big part of my success, because they gave me greater flexibility in making career decisions, and more peace of mind that our kids were always in the best hands possible—Mom's. As a result, my success is our success, which we enjoy together.

19. Isn't it just possible that what works for you won't work for others?
Yes, but if it works for some, it's worth the effort.

20.What's your next dream?
Read the next chapter!

10

My Next Dream

Little Faces

As she lay there in her mother's arms,
She was only a few minutes old.
My baby daughter had just had a baby girl,
A precious new member of a great big world.

My baby daughter said, "Would you like to hold
her?"
Of course I said yes, as my smile grew bolder.
As I picked her up with a gentle touch,
She was small, so fragile, and yet so much.

She had gone back to sleep after the struggle to
start her life.
Baby and Mommy were fine, everything was all
right.
When I looked at that little face, sent from God
above,
It was truly the face of a miracle, and of God's
divine love.

For a moment, I didn't know who I was or
where,
I could only think of her and so happy to be
there.
Born into the world with all the other little faces,
What will we do, to make it a better place?
                                    —The Hermanator

My Next Dream

On Wednesday, January 20, 1999, while attending a National Restaurant Association board meeting in Maui, Hawaii, I received a call from my wife Gloria. Our daughter Melanie, she said, was about to have her baby, so Gloria would be flying from Omaha to Atlanta that day to be with her.

I told Gloria that I would finish my meeting in Hawaii and head to Atlanta, also, but that I would probably not arrive before Melanie delivered her baby, since I had an important, previously scheduled "get-acquainted" meeting on Friday in Austin, Texas with then-Governor George W. Bush. I got to Austin on Thursday and stayed overnight, as planned. I continually called Gloria to make sure everything with Melanie was going normally, and to find out if I had become a granddad yet.

On Thursday, Melanie was experiencing severe labor pains, so Gloria and Melanie's husband, Cesare, took her to see her doctor. The doctor thought it was false labor, but told her if the pain persisted to go to the hospital. The pain did persist, so they went to the hospital where the attending nurse suggested that she go home! Gloria's motherly instincts told her that Melanie was in too much pain to go home and she insisted that

Melanie be admitted to the hospital. Throughout the rest of that day and into Friday, I was still calling in for frequent updates.

After my meeting on Friday afternoon, which lasted until 4:00 PM, I rushed to the Austin airport to catch the first non-stop flight to Atlanta. I arrived in Atlanta at about 9:00 PM, rented a car, and drove to the hospital, arriving there at 9:30. My son, Vincent, was in the waiting room, and he told me that the baby had not arrived yet, but that everything was still going okay.

At 9:56 PM, Celena Patrice came into this world. A few minutes later, Gloria came out and told Vincent and me, "We have a granddaughter, and Vincent has a niece." We were excited, but Gloria wore a somewhat exasperated look on her face.

When I asked what was bothering her, she explained, "I have been with this girl for three days, going back and forth to the hospital. I have been in the delivery room with her, dealing constantly with hospital personnel. And then you show up and the baby is born."

I told her that Celena was just waiting on Granddad before making her appearance. Gloria said, "I know, and I will have to hear this story for the rest of my life."

A few minutes later, I was allowed into the delivery room. Melanie was doing fine, a small blanket wrapping the new bundle in her arms. I smiled as I looked at Melanie and said, "My baby daughter has a baby daughter." Melanie, a big smile on her face, asked me if I wanted to hold my new granddaughter. Of course I did!

When I took Celena in my arms and looked at that tiny, fifteen-minute-old face, the first thought that ran through my mind was not, "How do we give her a better start in life?" as our parents had done for us, and we had done for our children. My first thought was, "How do I make this a better world?"

A Better World

During those moments as I looked at Celena's little face, I thought about all the other little faces around the world, and the kind of world we would leave them. My past dreams and accomplishments seemed small in comparison to the many challenges we face as a nation, and as a world of nations.

In the last one hundred years, we have eliminated many diseases from the face of the earth, and yet some diseases still threaten to wipe out entire nations.

Agricultural technology has given us the ability to produce more than enough food to feed every person on earth, but social and political barriers have prevented us from winning the war on hunger.

Computer technology has put a world of knowledge and information at our fingertips, yet our relative ability to educate the masses has decreased.

Despite all of the science, technology, and knowledge the world has developed, some people still lack the compassion and wisdom to cease senseless atrocities against other human beings.

Disease, hunger, and atrocities against other human beings are not just problems on the world stage. They are also unsolved problems in this, the world's greatest country.

Our national prosperity has enhanced the lifestyles and standard of living for millions of people, but millions of people still suffer from preventable diseases, and from hunger, and are the victims of violent atrocities.

Government programs to address these problems have made an attempt, but have failed to make a lasting impact, due to the escalating inefficiency of bureaucracy.

If the greatest country in the world does not produce the leadership to be CEO of Nations, then what will all the little faces inherit? The CEO of Nations must be a leadership nation of CEOs of SELF, whose compassionate people make a difference in their own lives and in the lives of others. Everyone is blessed with different abilities, but with the same ability to dream. When we choose to take charge as CEO of SELF, we allow ourselves to dream, we empower ourselves to be happy, and we use our God-given abilities to make a difference in the lives of others, and in the world.

My next dream is to make this a better world with the talents and time that God has given me. For whatever reason, I am blessed to have achieved all of my "decade goals" twenty years ahead of schedule. I do not know how much time I will have, or exactly how I am supposed to help all those little faces. But I know I must try and I will.

It's not my will, but Thy will be done.